African American Healthy Self-Esteem

T0158870

African American Healthy Self-Esteem

Understanding why low self esteem in African Americans occur and how to elevate Self-Esteem

Ramone Smith

iUniverse, Inc.
Bloomington

African American Healthy Self-Esteem
Understanding why low self esteem in African
Americans occur and how to elevate Self-Esteem

iUniverse books may be ordered through booksellers or by contacting:

iUniverse
1663 Liberty Drive
Bloomington, IN 47403
www.iuniverse.com
1-800-Authors (1-800-288-4677)

ISBN: 978-1-4620-4996-7 (sc)
ISBN: 978-1-4620-4997-4 (ebk)

Printed in the United States of America

iUniverse rev. date: 08/20/2011

Dedicated to my Late brother Glen Smith

Preface

As a black man born and raised in the urban ghetto of America, my life was unpredictable and difficult growing up. I can still remember many of my earliest childhood experiences, and at that time, I thought life would be a lot simpler. I had my mother, Joyce; my oldest brother, Glen; and my baby brother, Parrish, in my life. I felt loved and connected with my family. My father, Tommy, was not a very responsible man; however, I knew who he was, and he periodically came to the house. His visits were not necessarily to see my younger brother and myself, his biological children. He came primarily to see my mother, to satisfy his sexual urges. That might explain why I always called my father by his first name, never Dad.

Nonetheless, I can remember a few times when he would pick me up from kindergarten and hold my hand as we walked back to my mother's apartment. I must admit it was a bit confusing why he never stayed long with us. But at that age, I thought it was a normal family relationship and my self-esteem was high. My sense of self-worth was innately strong because as a youngster my world centered around my family, as if we were the only people on the planet.

Then some strange things began to occur as I started growing older. When my father came by, he and my mother would often get into fights. Sometimes they would even become violent, though at the time, I did not know why they were fighting. I now realize they were fighting because of my father's unwillingness to take responsibility as a parent. Also around this time my mother no longer had her job at the post office and went on welfare to financially support her three young boys. Incidentally we were on welfare for more than fifteen years. Money was very limited, and I remember my mother always being angry, frustrated, and impatient with us. The emotional conditions of my family changed, and subsequently so did my emotional well-being.

I remember it like it was yesterday. I was three years old, watching *The Brady Bunch* and noting how stable that white family appeared to be. They lived in a big house, had both parents together, and seemed to have enough resources to abundantly accommodate everyone. Mentally I contrasted this with my reality of our small apartment, instability, and of course a prominent family member missing. I remember saying to my brother Glen, "I wish I were white." I did not realize it at the time, but my self-esteem was taking a deep plunge that would continue in a downward spiral throughout most of my life.

My story is not unique; unfortunately, it is almost the norm for a large percentage of blacks born in urban American neighborhoods. As a result, many of us grow up confused, afraid, and uncertain about our abilities, partly because our families are fragmented and we haven't been taught the right tools we need to navigate our lives in a sometimes hostile environment. Subsequently, as adults we continuously make bad choices that have negative consequences and ultimately dictate the direction of our lives; all too often they have tragic outcomes.

I was fortunate. Older, positive black people always seemed to take a liking to me, offering advice and guidance. Perhaps I was actively looking for a father figure on some subconscious level, but I was not aware of it. By the time I was seventeen, I had committed several petty crimes for money.

One night I was arrested for disorderly conduct and was sentenced to probation for a year. My probation officer was a black man named Stephen Chandler, and he asked me two questions: Are you still in school? Do you have any children? At the time I was in school but was failing miserably. Also, I was fortunate enough not to have been a teenage father. Mr. Chandler simply responded, "There is still hope for you."

It was not easy, but I changed my life and subsequently achieved several accomplishments, including a master's degree in political science from Long Island University. However, despite all of my apparent success, I continued to suffer from low self-esteem. I thought that my academic success would eradicate that feeling of ineptness, but it continued throughout my life.

Finally, after a period of uncertainty about my employment status and the direction with my life, I bought a book on how to enhance self-esteem. I was depressed and thought it might offer something I did not already know. The book is titled, 'Maximum Self Esteem' by Jerry Minchinton, had a strong impact on me, and over time I gradually improved my self-esteem. The book explained that the concept of self-esteem is a learned behavior, and our life experiences play a significant role in its health. Also, it maintained that in order to increase self-esteem, we must be willing to do the internal work of self analysisnd sometimes this process can be painful and may include professional assistance such as therapy and counseling.

Since reading that initial self-esteem book, I have done a lot of research on the subject. I find the entire concept of self-esteem fascinating. As human beings we need a sufficient level of it to function effectively in society. I read several excellent books such as Minchinton's and 'Self Esteem' by Mathew Mckay and Patrick Fanning, on the topic by very conscientious people—however I started thinking that there was something missing.

Of all the races and ethnic groups that presently live in America, African Americans far and wide have the most unique history. We did not choose to come to this country of our free will; we were kidnapped from our homeland in Africa. Slavery was an American and European business practice for four hundred years, and only today are international world bodies tacitly acknowledging that it was an enormous crime against humanity.

The physical part of being human chattel was difficult enough for our ancestors. However, there was the psychological trauma that continues to persist since the

American 1865 emancipation from this institution. Finally, a lily white American society with its legacy of racism and discrimination was all but willing to fully include us as equals, despite our ability to adapt to our new homeland. Simply put, those variables had a very distinctive effect on African Americans and American society as a whole.

After Reconstruction in the late nineteenth century, a wave of new immigrants from Southern and Central Europe arrived at America's shores. These groups included the Poles, Russians, and the Italians. With great respect I acknowledge that these groups had a very difficult time in their efforts to assimilate and fully be accepted in American society. They faced intense ethnic prejudice and discrimination during their first few generations in this country—specifically the Italian Americans, who took almost seven generations to assimilate and at one time were targets themselves for lynchings in the early twentieth century.

Nonetheless these groups eventually assimilated into the American mainstream because they were white, and appearance could more easily be acculturated. According to *Strangers to These Shores* by renowned sociologist Dr. Vincent Parrillo, "humans are attracted to people who resemble to us . . . Numerous studies have explored the extent to which a person likes others because of similar attitudes, values, beliefs, social status, or physical appearance. Examining the development of attraction among people who are initially strangers to one another, an impressive number of these studies have found a positive relationship between the similarity of two people and their liking for each other. Most significantly, the findings show that people's perception of similarity between themselves is a more powerful determinant than actual similarity." Based on that assertion, I conclude that one of the reasons African Americans are still not fully accepted by American society is because of our skin color. Although the other white immigrant groups had a hard time, they were able to assimilate because eventually they successfully blended into the Anglo-Saxon construct of race acceptance.

America is very race and class conscious, and oftentimes the two go hand in hand. The Southern and Central European groups were able to enter into mainstream society because their skin, hair, and facial features were very similar to what was the standard of beauty and acceptance in America. As people of the African race, African Americans are essentially the opposite of this standard. Parrillo has a strong argument when he asserts that perception of similarities is more powerful than the actual similarity.

As further evidence to this assertion, in the January 3 editorial section of the *New York Daily News,* Ben Krull wrote an article about adoption in New York. Mr. Krull, a family court lawyer, addressed the point that affluent whites are more likely to adopt a foreign Asian or Latin American child than an underprivileged African American. "It's common to see white couples in Manhattan's affluent neighborhoods pushing strollers with an Asian or Hispanic child inside. But I rarely come across mixed-race families formed around African American children . . . This is a situation that threatens to worsen the sense of alienation in New York's black community because they see new immigrant groups accepted by white New York in ways that they are not."

It is not absurd to conclude that because Asian or Hispanic children possess light skin, they will be more accepted for generations to come and will eventually benefit from what America has to offer in terms of opportunities. Native-born black children, due to the high visibility of dark skin, will have their humanity much less acknowledged, and they will have far less life-improving opportunities in future generations. Being born black in America, particularly dark skinned, is an automatic disadvantage that white society refuses to acknowledge because it is not a part of their frame of reference or reality construct. Also, neither of these groups faced the horror of being slaves in this country, or having race coded barriers in the form of segregation aimed exclusively against them. With the exception of the Chinese Exclusion Act of 1882, no other ethnic group had race-based discriminatory laws passed against them in this country to legally bar them from assimilation. When these groups arrived, they did so of their own free will and brought with them their native language, culture, and religion.

During the institution of slavery, blacks were forced to this country and were denied the human right to practice any indigenous customs. Our sense of reality from Africa was wiped clean from our collective psyche and replaced with a socialized inferiority complex that equated power with white skin and the lack thereof with being black; this concept has been perpetuated and continues to exist today. As African Americans, this continues to put us at a physical and psychological disadvantage. The American socialization process teaches us that almost everything that is associated with being white has a positive connotation, and everything black is the least desired opposite. Even things as subtle as angel food cake and devil's food cake, or black attire at funerals and white at weddings. The very basis of American social ideology is a direct assault on our self-esteem.

Due to the African American's distinctive history, and because of my strong grasp on how important self-esteem is, I felt it was necessary to write a self-esteem book aimed specifically at African Americans. Nonetheless I want to make something clear about this endeavor. Although polemic for some, this book is not about being angry, assessing blame, or promoting a victim's response to today's modern challenges. However, the historical context is significant because in order to discuss self-esteem, we must take a clinical look at the conditions that helped create it.

In addition, although poor self-esteem clearly affects all racial or ethnic groups, my target for discussion is African Americans due to our history and subsequent special needs in order to enhance our sense of self-worth. This work focuses on asserting ideas aimed at personal empowerment and reclaiming that lost value as a human being that makes us worthy of love and respect.

In addition, I argue that black men suffer from low self-esteem more than black women because even though black women suffer just as much from low self-esteem, to their credit they at least operate on a level of basic functioning in society. Statistically they attain higher academic and vocational achievements than African American men. Sadly African American men comprise an overwhelming number of those that are caught up in the criminal justice system, making up more than 80 percent of the prison population in America. According to Wikipedia's 'Racial inequality in the American

Criminal Justice System, "the likelihood of black males going to prison in their lifetime is 16% compared to 2% of white males and 9% of Hispanic males".'This is quite alarming in light of the fact that African Americans are only 14 percent of the total US population. In New York City alone, the unemployment rate for black men exceeds 50 percent. More that half of all black children will be born into single-parent households. A significant number of black men will have long-term battles with alcohol and substance abuse, or commit domestic violence and child abuse. And finally, according to the Center for Disease Control and Prevention or CDC located in Dekalb County in Atlanta Georgia, African American males are seven times as likely to be diagnosed with HIV than white men. Again, African Americans are only 14 percent of the population but account for almost 50 percent of all HIV/AIDS cases in America. Clearly, this is the behavior of a segment of society that collectively says, "I don't care what happens to me."

With these statistics, it is clear that some African Americans are making very disturbing and difficult choices that are based on the reality of their circumstances. I worked in the criminal justice system for a time and had the opportunity to witness this form of self-destructive behavior up close. The prevailing attitude with many young African American men is that there is no hope or chance for a better life; therefore they live for the moment without thinking about the consequences of their actions. This attitude relates to a self-esteem problem. I firmly believe that if someone can learn to accept and love himself or herself unconditionally, the likelihood of making better life decisions increases. The entire premise of having strong self-esteem enables a person to think about the future, make better decisions, and take responsibility for one's life. Therefore I attribute many of the African Americans problems to poor self-esteem.

I am aware of the efforts of black academics that have researched African history, which includes the great Egyptian civilization. Eyewitness accounts from the Greek philosopher Plato, the facial features carvings on the statues, and DNA testing have confirmed that they were of the African race. Also our own rich history here in America, including our contributions to technology, culture, and the arts, are widely appreciated, even if they are not always adequately taught in schools and universities.

Nonetheless, the history of American black people has been and continues to be recorded by extraordinary people. However even the most glorious of history lessons can fail to positively impact one's self-esteem for two reasons. First, it is in the past, and it's not productive to live in or try to re-create the past. It can be an inept approach to effectively dealing with life today; your given right to be happy with who you are is your responsibility within the reality of this epoch. Second, racial and ethnic pride at best can have only a superficial effect on raising someone's self-esteem. Each person is unique and has unique experiences that contribute greatly to how one views oneself. We can take pride in the fact that Michael Jordan, Dr. Ben Carson, Reginald Lewis, Johnny Cochran, Bill Cosby, and Mohammed Ali are African American, but their achievements are inconsequential to every single black man's life. Therefore exaggerated forms of ethnic pride are insufficient solutions to genuine self-esteem for the individual.

Having good self-esteem means that despite being born into difficult circumstances, you are still a valuable member of the human race and have the power control the direction and the outcome of your life. You have the tools to feel good about yourself, even when things are not going well in your life. I believe that everyone has the ability to change life's patterns if one truly wants to. I am living proof that it can be done. Therefore with this book, I challenge you, the reader, to learn how to increase your personal self-worth and live a more conscious life committed to being the best person you can be. Yesterday's mistakes do not have to be one's destiny; they can serve as lessons for today.

Chapter One
Explaining What Self-Esteem Is

In order for to fully understand the concept we are dealing with, we must know what self-esteem is. As explained by Jerry Minchintin in his book *Maximum Self-Esteem,* "The nature of self-esteem is the value we place on our selves, our assessment of our worth as a human being." Nathaniel Branden in *The Six Pillars of Self-Esteem* goes a little deeper and writes that self-esteem is the "confidence in our ability to think, confidence in our ability to cope with the basic challenges of life . . . the confidence in our right to be successful and happy, the feeling of being worthy, deserving, entitled to assert our needs and wants, achieve our values, and enjoy the fruits of our efforts."

A healthy level of self-esteem allows us to trust in our mental abilities to make the best decisions under any circumstances. Self-esteem is how we feel about ourselves. It gives us permission to be happy with who we are without feeling guilty. It governs our awareness about who we are and gives us a sense of purpose. It continuously reminds us to think and act on the behalf of our natural right to self-preservation. In many respects self-esteem is the practice of appropriate decision making in order to successfully navigate our lives.

For example, African Americans growing up in an urban milieu with high self-esteem would make the decision to avoid experimenting with illicit drugs, perform well in school, practice protected sex, and not allow themselves to be influenced by negative peer pressure. They accepts themselves unconditionally and understand that their decisions trigger consequences; poor decision making can lead to undesirable consequences. I will elaborate later on about the idea of decision making because this is a very important component to self-esteem.

Self-esteem is taking responsibility for the decisions one makes and accepting the consequences. If a man decides to have unprotected sex with a woman he recently met, he does not blame her if she becomes pregnant or if he contracts a sexually transmitted disease. Self-esteem is the ability to forgive oneself for making mistakes and to avoid sliding into deprecating levels of self-loathing.

Self-esteem gives us the ability and confidence to learn new information and skills that allow us to adapt and become marketable in an ever-changing world. Without a healthy level of self-esteem, most people seek to avoid new knowledge and in effect render themselves stagnant in the pursuit of progress.

This may appear as a simple exercise to execute, however based on the statistics listed in the preface, it is clear that in reality this task is more difficult to pull off.

Jerry Minchinton asserts that there are three aspects to self-esteem.

Aspect one is how we feel about ourselves.

> With *high self-esteem*, we accept ourselves unconditionally exactly as we are; we appreciate our value as a human being. When we have *low self-esteem,* we believe we have little intrinsic worth. We believe our personal value is in direct proportion to the value of our accomplishments.

> Some of us try too hard and become highly competitive workaholics and over-achievers. With few genuine of self-worth, we try to create some and prove we are somebody by our successes and achievements. Because our desire for perfection is so great, we set unrealistic goals and place unreasonable demands on ourselves. Failing rather than encouraging us to have more realistic aspirations, only leads to a more punishing round of self-blame and a resolve to drive ourselves harder next time. If we do finally achieve our goals, we are disappointed; despite everything we have done, we still empty inside.

> Poor self—esteem makes some of us afraid to try. When we under value our work, and ourselves we doubt our abilities and are often afraid to ask for the raise or advancement we deserve. If our feelings of self-worth

are limited, we place strict limitations on what we can accomplish.

We consider ourselves of little importance, both personally and to others. We are excessively demanding when we judge ourselves; too critical of our actions, we continually berate ourselves for real or imagined flaws.

Vulnerable to the opinions of others, we desperately try to gain their recognition and approval, sometimes through risky and dangerous behavior. Or we may try to impress them by associating with the "right" people earning the "right" degrees, having the "right" jobs, driving the "right kind of car, and living in the "right" neighborhood. Our desire for praise and special acknowledgment is endless. Failing to get the recognition we feel should be ours, we become angry and hurt.

We are at the mercy of our emotions: instead of controlling them, we permit them to control us. Since we allow circumstances to influence our feelings, we are inclined to be moody. The insecurity we feel as a result of devaluing ourselves makes us react with jealously, envy and possessiveness. Fear makes us greedy and acquisitive, and feelings of self-hate alternate with those of futility, unhappiness, and depression. Please add as a foot note: Jerry Minchinton, Maximum Self Esteem, Anford House Publishers, copyright 1993:

I will broaden aspect one and correlate it specifically to blacks. As black people with high self-esteem, we accept ourselves based on the principle that we are living organisms that have a right to exist on this planet. We accept our skin color, hair texture, facial features, and varying body types without apology. Living in this Western Civilization—centered reality is difficult. However, with high self-esteem we are not adversely affected psychologically by the images with which we are inundated. How we view ourselves is independent of the depictions from magazines on what is a good-looking or successful man.

A black person with high self-esteem feels comfortable and good about his existence, no matter what challenge he faces. If he is the victim of a racial attack, whether verbal, social, or physical, he does not feel unworthy, inept, or sorry that he was born into a race that is still struggling for recognition. He does not feel guilty and understands that the fault lies within the perpetrators of the biased crime, not in him.

Black people with high self-esteem value their uniqueness and the fact that our appearance, culture and artistic interest are different from mainstream American society. There is no succumbing to social pressures that attempt to dictate what are the appropriate cultural, social, and artistic interests to have. We are happy being ourselves and following our interests, whatever they may be. We accept the things we can do and the things we cannot. In most cases our interests dictate our choices of educational and vocational pursuits. However, our capabilities, along with a certain level of commitment, determine how successful we may be in those endeavors. With high self-esteem, we do not allow our successes—or more importantly our failures—to set the barometer for our self-worth.

A black person with high self-esteem has self-respect and is very conscientious of the decisions he makes. For example, a young man from an urban environment has a goal to attend the best university for his academic abilities. He understands that he has to do his best in high school, and this oftentimes requires social sacrifices that can lead to peer ridicule. Other teenagers who tease him and say he is acting white by getting good grades and wanting to secure a prosperous future do not affect his ability to focus. For the teenager who is not as confident and is still looking for social and peer acceptance, this is a precarious dilemma. Studies have revealed that black teenagers are more susceptible to peer influence than any other group. Therefore when he learns to elevate his self-esteem, he also increases his self-respect and is not affected by the insults. He is in control of his emotions and accepts the fact that he is his own person; he chooses the direction for his life.

As I alluded to earlier in the preface, my own self-esteem was severely challenged. During my high school years, I found myself getting into a great deal of trouble: numerous fights, drug experimentation, and skipping school altogether. I finally dropped out of school at the age of eighteen, and I was still in the tenth grade. My self-esteem was very poor, and this made me easy prey for negative peer pressure. I wanted to fit in and be accepted by my "friends" and would do almost anything they suggested. Getting high, riding in stolen cars, and performing robberies were just a few of the ideas that they had. I never went out with my friends to steal cars, but when they had them, I would ride with, and we would smoke marijuana while parked on some isolated street. Even though I was high off of the reefer, I would always make an excuse and get out of the car before it was time to drive off somewhere. I was fortunate that I never got caught inside a stolen vehicle. I do remember committing an unarmed robbery and being arrested by a racist police officer who gratuitously used the N-word. That was my third robbery, and up until that point, my jobs had been successes. Nonetheless, I was sixteen, and that would not be the last time I sat in a cell.

In retrospect I now understand that most of my bad choices during my high school years were made because of low self-esteem, and my home life was not conducive to healthy self-esteem. I have since learned that the home is the first influence on self-esteem, and based on the level of parental functioning, this could encourage or discourage healthy self-esteem growth. I will get into the role of parents on self-esteem later.

Jerry Minchinton's second aspect to self-esteem is our feelings about life.

"When we have High self-esteem, we accept responsibility for and have a feeling of control over every part of our lives".

> "We have a comfortable acceptance of reality; we do not blame it on our problems. We set attainable goals and have realistic expectations. We hold ourselves responsible for what occurs in our lives and believe that ultimately, what happens to us occurs primarily because of our choices and decisions, rather than outside factors. Because we realize we have the power to alter them as we choose. While we are willing to consider others opinions about how to conduct our lives, we

have chosen to be our own final authority, to give the greatest weight to our own ideas of what is right and best for us.

The control we exercise is not control over others, or even necessarily over circumstances, but over ourselves and our reactions and responses. We change the circumstances to suite us when it is appropriate and change our attitude about them when it is not".

I remember reading Stephen Covey's book *The 7 Habits of Highly Successful People.* He asserted that it is not the situation or the problem that makes us feel bad; it is the way in which we react to the circumstance that hurts us. In spite of the challenges he faces daily, a black person with high self-esteem has a sense that he is in control of his life. Most of us have seen many cases in which it is apparent that several black men do not have this feeling of control over their lives.

A black man with high self-esteem looks at his life and accepts the circumstances that determine his reality; he knows he is at a social, political, and economic disadvantage because he is black. However, this does not limit his aspirations in attaining certain goals and subsequently creating his own reality. He is responsible and understands that the circumstances of his life are the result of his decisions; external conditions such as racism and discrimination can affect his reality, but he is cognizant of the fact of how he reacts.

When we have high self-esteem, we trust our thinking process. We will encounter people who are always willing to offer advice on what course of action we should take in light of a given situation. The advisers may not have a strong sense of who they are. This is especially important within the black community because of the heavy influence of peer pressure that continues to exist. A black man with healthy self-esteem may consider other people's advice, but he ultimately knows the decision is his.

All too often we can be unhappy with our lives and the direction it has taken based on past decisions. A black person with high self-esteem will view this situation as an opportunity and give himself the power to change his reality. There is a clear understanding of recognizing we do not control all circumstances; neither do we control, or need to control, the players involved. What we do control is ourselves and making the best decisions within that circumstance.

For example, a twenty-five-year-old black male is released from prison after completing a four-year debt to society; he is on parole for the next five or six years. He did not complete high school and has limited mobility restrictions within his parole status. He does not control the circumstances (i.e. parole), but he can set attainable goals while he is under state control. Ideally he should change his viewpoint of life and conscientiously decide against any further interaction with old street acquaintances. He should seek to attain a GED, try to if economically feasable or through finacial aide, enter into college, and at least complete the curriculum for a BA degree. By this time he would have fulfilled his parole requirements and would now be on his way to becoming a productive member of society. Also, by attaining some form of high academic credentials, this can reduce the probibility of employment rejection based on being a convicted felon.

After dropping out of school in the tenth grade, I attained my GED in the spring of 1987. I passed the exam on my first attempt, and after an academic season in the transitional year program at Brandeis University, I was accepted to St. Augustine's College, a black school in Raleigh, North Carolina. I remember how excited I was when I first told my former street partner that I was going to college in North Carolina. Up until that point we had not seen much of each other due to my GED and Brandeis University commitments. After revealing my educational plans, he looked at me oddly, and instead of congratulating me, he said, "You're not going to make it." He also took the liberty to explain why I would fail in my pursuit of a college education. For someone with poor self-esteem, his argument would have been convincing and subsequently would have had a negative impact on my decision to go to college. However at that time my self-esteem was very high, and I had a great deal of confidence in my academic potential. His argument failed as he tried persuading me not to go to North Carolina. Instead I was actually quite hurt by it, wondering why my best friend would not want to see me succeed in life.

I now understand that his response had nothing directly to do with me. As confident and street savvy as he was, he was struggling with his own failure to complete high school. In addition, seeing someone who came from the same ghetto actively pursue a college education only made him feel worse about the direction of his own life. His self-esteem was very low, and he did not know how to take personal responsibility. Instead he projected his anger at himself onto me.

Jerry Minchinton's third aspect to self-esteem is our relationships.

> "With high self-esteem, we have a tolerance of and respect for all people, along with the belief that they are entitled to the same rights we wish for ourselves.
>
> When we are comfortable with our selves, we respect people's right to be as they are, do as they choose, and live as they see fit, as long as they are willing to extend the same courtesy to us and others. We do not try to force our values or beliefs on people because we don't need their acceptance to make us feel worthy.
>
> We are reasonable, accepting of others' short-comings, even tempered, flexible, and responsible in our relationships. We see all persons as equally worthy and equally deserving of respect. The idea that one person can be inherently more worthwhile that another is inconsistent with the principles of high self-esteem".

Similar to the majority culture, the black community is equipped with its own internal social strata. This tacitly acknowledged caste system has existed for years and provides the social distance that economically successful blacks desire in order to not be recognized within the stereotypical images of lower class blacks. Understand this point: there is nothing wrong with attaining the resources to living a better life. In fact that is the goal of most blacks. However many successful blacks confuse status achievements with high self-esteem and maintain a condescending viewpoint toward blacks that are still struggling in the urban communities.

When a black high school teacher is unable to effectively educate a class of public school black children because of her own personal value system and biases, and she subsequently ridicules or insults them, she is the person with the self-esteem problem. She has the mistaken belief that perhaps her personal circumstances, such as a stable home with two parents, allowed her to achieve a good education and that her students are enjoying the same social luxury. In addition, because of her students' apparent apathy toward education, she concludes that she is better than they are because she has a master's degree. A similar phenomenon exists when well-off blacks look down at or are patronizing to homeless people or drug addicts.

Feeling superior to those that are less fortunate than you are is incongruent with a healthy self-esteem. Although a black person is by no means obligated to help or contribute money or services to others, developing a superficial sense of superiority toward someone who may not have had the advantages is not consistent with the idea of high self-esteem.

Also, the black community is absolutely notorious for its opposition to homosexuality. This is an ideology that is consistent throughout the world, however with perhaps the exception of the American Latino community, the black community historically has been more intolerant of homosexuality, in particular black gay men and the perception of their sexual behavior and role in the black community. Much of the homophobia philosophy is rooted in Christianity, which is a significant part of black American socialization and culture. I will discuss the relationship between religion and self-esteem later in the text.

Low self-esteem limits one's scope and acceptance of other human beings' chosen lifestyle. A person does not have to agree with it, much like a Democrat may not agree with the political perception of a staunch Republican. Nonetheless, a person with high self-esteem treats everyone with the same respect, without feeling uncomfortable or concerned with how others may perceive him. I will admit this is a continued struggle with the black community.

My oldest brother Glen died of AIDS on October 25, 2002, ten days after my thirty-sixth birthday. My brother was an openly gay black man, and I can remember how socially difficult it was growing up with this open family secret. As I mentioned in the preface, due to my family's fragmentation and economic conditions, we were always on the brink of emotional chaos. During a time in my life when we particularly doing bad, my mother received a call from an acquaintance that knew someone who had seen Glen at a gay nightclub. The caller informed my mother that Glen was dancing and carrying on with another man. After hanging up, my mother became uncontrollably upset and started crying and yelling at Glen to tell her whether it was true. Glen was visibly shaken and did not directly answer her. While my younger brother and I were crying ourselves, we tried to calm my mother down.

I will never forget how the three of us, out of our ignorance, ganged up and condemned him. Prior to that call we suspected that he was gay, but because of our poor family self-esteem, we were willing to be in denial about the subject. Prior to this, Glen a nervous breakdown and spent several months at an in-patient mental health hospital. Years later my mother told me that he broke down because he was struggling with his sexual orientation. This happened in1982 and I was in the ninth grade. I was very aware of my image among my friends in terms of having a faggot for a big brother. Because of my low self-esteem and general selfishness, I did not acknowledge what had to be an incredible amount of internal personal pain that my brother was going through. In effect I turned my back on him because I was more concerned about what the community, in particular my friends, would think of me. If my self-esteem had been healthy at that time, I would not have treated my very own flesh and blood indifferently. Furthermore, I am convinced that if Glen's self-esteem was healthy, he would have accepted being gay, not concerned himself with the stigma, and made better lifestyle decisions that would not have put his life in jeopardy. I would argue that he would be alive today if he had learned the principles of high self-esteem and applied them to his life.

When we improve our self-esteem, our entire outlook on the world becomes different. As illustrated by Jerry Minchinton, when our self-esteem is low, we view the world as a cold, hostile, and uncaring place. This is particularly true for black men, as evidenced by the antisocial behavior that many young men practice.

Due to the historical reference of discrimination that continues generation after generation, black men have been socialized to perceive the world as very dangerous, and they maintain a sense of safeness within their community, mentally limiting themselves. Their innate curiosity is inhibited by the fear of being denied, discriminated against, or in extreme cases assaulted by the majority culture. This is demonstrated by Vincent Parillo in his concept "The Vicious Circle Phenomenon," which addresses "the dynamics of the inter-group relations where prejudice and discrimination serve as reciprocal stimuli and responses to reinforce one another." In essence, society discriminates against black men, and black men feel deprecated, lashing out and behaving in a way that encourages more discrimination from society.

Another explanation is the fear-based socialization process inculcated by the black mother toward her sons. Since slavery black mothers actively raised their sons differently than their daughters, whether they were aware of it or not. The theory goes that the world is not very kind to uppity black men with intelligence and strong personalities who don't know "their place" in society. Black mothers, through their own fear of the world, raised their sons to be psychologically equipped with internal alarms that warned them not to overexpress themselves emotionally and to stay within a tacit parameter of safety. This way they would not pose a threat to the white slave master and subsequently would not be in harm's way. Sociological evidence suggests that this fear-based mother-son teaching has been perpetuated into contemporary society. In addition, Nathaniel Brandon refers to this phenomenon as "a retardation of the separation and evolution into individuation. This occurs when children fail to achieve a normal level of maturity because either their parents were unequipped with the tools to foster and facilitate healthy separation, or the children refuse to attain maturity for fear of growing up and taking on responsibility".

Although black mothers feel they are protecting their sons, unfortunately in some cases they are sabotaging their sons' natural abilities to transcend inhibitions and explore the world in a healthy and rewarding manor. Incidentally, this has had a serious impact on the black man's self-esteem and the perspective in which he views the world. This can also help to explain some of the psychosis of poor decision making that can lead to a precarious lifestyles.

Conversely, when our self-esteem is high, we view the world as filled with opportunities, and the setbacks we experience in life are merely lessons to help us better navigate it. I argue that most black men want to change their lives for the better—they just do not have the tools to do so.

Jerry Minchinton asserts that "sound self-esteem is the basis for all improvement."

> "As human beings, our potential is limitless, our abilities inexhaustible, and the possibilities for creative and constructive change are endless. But, we won't experience satisfactory progress towards our goals or make any lasting improvements, unless we believe we deserve the good we want. Just wanting more out of life in not enough; we must first give our selves permission to have it. If we fail to, then no amount of changes will make us happier. Regardless of how many wonderful events take place in our lives or how fortunate we are in other ways, unless we believe we deserve to have and enjoy the good that comes our way, it will slip through

our fingers, or we will fail to appreciate it because we don't believe we genuinely merit it".

Because of the low self-esteem that many of us black men have, we innately feel undeserving of good fortune and certain opportunities. We therefore sabotage the good that is happening to us. We have to learn to embrace and assert the fact that we are just as deserving of a good and permanent existence as anyone else. Kool Moe Dee made one of the most profound statements in the movie *Panther*: "I think poor white people are fighting for more money, and black people are fighting for their humanity!"

Chapter Two
The Genesis of Poor Self-Esteem

The presence of the blacks is the greatest evil that threatens the United States. They increase in the Gulf States, faster than do the whites. They cannot be kept forever in slavery, since the tendencies of the modern world run strongly the other way. They cannot be absorbed into the white population, for the whites will not intermarry with them, not even in the North where they have been free for two generations. Once freed, they would be more dangerous than now, because they would not long submit to be debarred from political rights. A terrible struggle would ensue.

These are the words of Mr. James Bryce, a pre-Civil War historian and US diplomat who was addressing an audience of Southern slaveholders about the status of the institution of slavery. This and other historical events are very significant to the eventual evolution of self-esteem in the African American.

In his book *The Six Pillars of Self-Esteem,* Nathaniel Brandon asserts that in earlier Western culture, individualism and personal self-esteem were discouraged in the name of the community. "In medieval times, the "self" as we understood the idea still lay sleeping in the human psyche. The basic mind-set was tribal, not individualistic. Each person was born into a distinct and unchangeable place in the social order. With very rare exceptions, one did not choose and occupation but rather was cast by circumstances of birth into the role peasant, artisan, or knight-or wife of one. One's sense of security derived, not from one's achievements, but from seeing oneself as an integral part of "the natural order," which was presumed to be ordained by God.

Our idea of the individual as an autonomous, self-determining unit, able to think independently and bearing responsibility for his or her existence emerged from several historical developments. The Renaissance in the fifteenth century, along with the reformation in the sixteenth, and the enlightenment in the eighteenth century. Also their two offspring, the Industrial Revolution and Capitalism. Self-esteem as we think about the concept today, has its roots in the post-Renaissance emerging culture of individualism.

Incidentally it was those two institutions, capitalism and the Industrial Revolution, that had a long-lasting, detrimental effect on African Americans. It was not the integrity of the events or the institutions themselves, but how white America historically used them to disenfranchise and exclude black America from the party.

The historical presence of African Americans can be described in five stages: slavery, the Emancipation Proclamation, Reconstruction, Jim Crow, and the civil rights movement.

Slavery

The first Africans to arrive in colony of Jamestown during the early seventeenth century were the lucky ones. They voluntarily came as indentured servants and secured labor jobs to work off their debts to the American sponsor who financed their voyage. After the contractual agreement of labor was completed, the Africans were freed and lived in colonial America uninhibited, enjoying the same rights as any other American. However, this labor-economic arrangement did not last long. At this time there were also white immigrants that served as indentured servants, and the plantation owners, along with the financial sponsors of indentured servitude, usually paid the exact amount of money to invest in the transportation and labor of a servant.

The proprietors of this institution soon realized that it would be much cheaper to have the Africans serve as slaves on a permanent basis. Understand the rationalization for this thinking. One of problems of white indentured servitude was that they could run away and blend into mainstream society, which resulted in a loss of productivity and money. Due to the high visibility of the Africans' skin color, if they ran away they did not have this luxury. Also, if the whites bought slaves, they no longer had to pay for the voyages of African immigrants to the colonies as they did for the white indentured servants. This gave rise to the new economic institution of slave shipbuilding, specifically for the purpose of transporting hundreds of men, women, and children from Africa. This in itself was a very lucrative industry because shipbuilding companies would manufacture slave ships for wealthy industrialists throughout the Americas, thus explaining how so many Africans arrived in all parts of the western hemisphere in such a short period of time.

The slave industrialists would simply sail to Africa and capture as many slaves as their ships could hold. Most of the time they would overpack because they knew they would lose a great deal of lives in transportation across the Atlantic. This methodology of cargo assembly was referred to as tightly packing.

Because of the enormous economic success of the slave trade, America was able to skip a socioeconomic period on its way to becoming fully developed capitalist. As asserted by Karl Marx, all industrial nations go through three stages of development: traditional, feudal, and capitalist. Unlike European nations, the United States went straight from traditional to full-blown capitalism. The reason is because the U.S. had two hundred years of free slave labor that permitted her to bypassed the necessity of feudalism. With the institution of slavery, proprietors of cotton, tobacco and other goods did not have to pay salaries and benefited from hundreds of free man power hours. Capitalist were able to retain most if not all of their invested money with little overhead to address. This causation helpped to eliminate the need for fuedalism.

On a personal note, I remember when I was in undergraduate studies, and I made this point in one of my sociology classes. The professor, who happened to be white, never provided a satisfactory retort. He neither confirmed nor denied that slavery played a significant role in America's socioeconomic developmental leap. The interesting thing was he was a self-proclaimed Marxist. However due to the cognitive dissonance from which many white people suffer, he was still unable to acknowledge the humanity of the forced and exploited African slaves' contribution to America's greatness.

In order for the institution of slavery to maintain stability, not only did it restrict the human rights of slaves physically, but it also included a process of mental dehumanization to prevent revolts or rebellions from the discontented slaves. This is very important in understanding the social-generational effect on the self-esteem of African Americans. As slaves African Americans were no different from cattle or any other animal for agricultural or industrial purposes. This is why the African American experience is different from other immigrant groups' social progress. Chattel slavery, the systematic denial of human rights, and no educational opportunities were all factors. In fact during slavery, it was a federal crime to teach a slave to read or write. African slaves were stripped of their original language and native customs and subsequently were unable to recreate any ethnocentric institutions that would allow them to make an easier transition in America. Other European immigrant groups were permitted to create ethnic enclaves and minicultural representations of their homeland when they willfully decided to come to the United States. For all intents and purposes, slavery started as an economic institution. However the legacy of race discrimination is the byproduct of that institution, and most countries in the

Americas are still dealing with it, even in the twenty-first century.

The problem I have with self-esteem authors is their failure to recognize the impact white racism had on the self-esteem of African Americans, particularly because they are so good at identifying how historical events can affect self-esteem and how a cultural Euro-centric reality sends negative messages to people of African descent. Two hundred years of master-slave relations undoubtedly affected the psychological development of both races.

Brandon asserts that an individual's self-esteem could not socially develop in Medieval Europe because people felt their position in life was the natural order, ordained by God. During and after slavery, white people felt the same way regarding their superior status toward blacks: God had chosen the white race to rule over the black race.

Emancipation Proclamation

American slavery officially ended in 1865 after the close of the Civil War. The issues surrounding the Civil War were that white Southerners wanted to maintain their slaveholding status, particularly because their agrarian economy depended on this institution. During this dispute they were unwilling to follow the North's lead in abolishing slavery. The North had abolished slavery as an economic institution two generations earlier, but despite this apparent act of morality, racial discrimination still continued to exist in the Southern states and the Northern states as well.

Rather than comply with the direction of the country, the Southern states seceded from the Union and created their own confederacy. In realty there were two countries at this point: the Union North, who was headed by President Abraham Lincoln, and the Confederate South, whose president was Jefferson Davis. The name of Davis is now obscure in most American history books, but nonetheless, he was a firm advocate of white supremacy and the separation of the races. President Lincoln would defeat the South and once again bring the Southern states back into the Union; he then initiated the process of eliminating slavery from those regions. However Jefferson Davis' ideology of race supremacy would continue to influence both the North and the South and for the next 150 years.

Reconstruction

During Reconstruction the federal union army occupied the now defeated Southern states to ensure the practice of releasing slaves and integrating them into mainstream society. Within one generation African Americans began to prosper at a rate that was phenomenal for any immigrant or racial group. African Americans took advantage of their new opportunities to become educators, politicians, and successful businesspeople.

The slave experience created a conditioned work ethic and strong aspirations toward any goals that were open for competition. As the first freeborn descendants of slaves, African Americans took their destinies in their own hands, and for a time it appeared that racial equality had a chance to develop in America. The concept of social distance as explained by Parillo had significantly decreased between the two races, and for blacks there was a feeling of inclusion.

Unfortunately, this did not last long; Reconstruction ended in 1876, and the federal government pulled its union troops out of the South. With no military protection, the South instituted a racially motivated social order known as the Black Codes. In addition, immigrants from Western Europe began to arrive in large numbers. These immigrants included Italians, Czechs, Poles, and Jews. As the Industrial Revolution rapidly developed factory jobs throughout the country, I hypothisize that the capitalist owners chose to use the newly arrived immigrants for their industrial factory labor—and in effect barred newly freed African American slaves from the possibility of employment. This action stymied what would have been an earlier establishment of the black middle/working class in the late nineteenth century.

Jim Crow

The Black Codes were very simple: the South revived the ideology of white supremacy and relegated African Americans to an inferior social status. Blacks were systematically disenfranchised by segregation, discriminated against for job selections in favor of newly arrived white immigrants, and occupationally evicted from land that was procured by honest means. The creation of separate civic and social institutions such as hospitals, public transportation, schools, and restaurants enforced and supported the imagined reality that whites by nature were superior to blacks.

Vincent Parrillo writes, "Economic problems, scandals and frustrations endured by southern whites appear to be some of the factors that reshaped their attitudes. In a region where they had long been considered inferior, many blacks were achieving socioeconomic respectability and becoming economic competitors. Resentment at black upward mobility, amplified by a historical undercurrent of racial attitudes, was further increased by economic troubles (declining cotton prices and unemployment). Because blacks were racially distinct, they became a convenient scapegoat for the frustrations and hostility of southern whites."

The South was able to reinstitute the racial status quo with no interference from the North because many believed that America's race problems were a "Southern issue." Because most African Americans lived in the South, the rest of the country felt that there wasn't a race problem due to their respective marginal black populations. Nonetheless, plebiscite racism and social discrimination continued to be a reality throughout all regions of the United States during this time. This is a reality that escapes the social consciousness of most of white America. Because of cognitive dissonance which is defined by Wikipedia as "the state of having inconsistent thoughts, beliefs, or attitudes, esp. as relating to behavioral decisions and attitude change", whites are unable to acknowledge the psychological impact of this type of social double standard. It's not just the race-based social practices that were supported for a century, but it is also the universal ideology of white skin privilege as a social status symbol that has hurt the African American psyche. Whites are immune to this effect because they are not the victims of a color-based society. In essence, they are in their natural psychological habitat, where an Euro-centric reality protects their subconscious and prevents it from looking outside that psychological defense mechanism construct. Their perspective of the world is subjective in the purest sense—that is, "If it didn't affect me, it didn't really happen."

We saw an example of this during the aftermath of Hurricane Katrina, in which several African American survivors testified before the US Senate that New Orleans police used excessive force as a means of maintaining social order. One unarmed black woman stated that police officers threatened her, along with children and elderly adults, with guns and profanity. After what she described as clearly a blatant violation of civil rights, a white Senate member dismissed her argument by simply responding, "I don't believe the police would act in that manner."

Civil Rights Movement

It's widely accepted that the modern civil rights movement began with the preplanned civil disobedience of Rosa Parks. In Montgomery, Alabama, in 1955, Parks sat in an empty seat at the back of the bus reserved for colored people. When a white man entered the bus, she was told to give up the seat by the bus driver. She refused and was arrested, thus setting off a wave of boycotts and protests that were successful in getting the federal court to overturn this supremacist-based practice. For the next ten years or so, just like with Reconstruction, the federal government used the military to enforce the assimilation of blacks into America's mainstream.

In Southern cities like Little Rock, Arkansas, the resistance to integration was so vehement that then Governor George Wallace used National Guard troops to preclude the impending social progress. This act of defiance prompted President Dwight D. Eisenhower to make the decision of exerting executive control over the state National Guard and putting them under US Army control. The Southern white supremacists were not happy about the social winds of change, and as the civil rights movement gained more momentum, they became increasingly powerless to derail it.

Out of the movement came an increasing awareness of civil and human rights. The strongest of these voices to advocate for black freedom were Martin Luther King Jr. and Malcolm X. Although they differed philosophically about how to attain civil and human rights, they were equally effective in initiating change for the social improvement for blacks in America. Both were courageous iconic figures that loved their people and were not afraid to sacrifice their lives for the cause. From Malcolm and Martin came the ideology of Black Power.

Several church and college-based groups, like the Southern Christian Leadership Conference (SCLC) and the Student Nonviolent Coordinating Committee (SNCC), began to initiate boycotts, sit-ins, and protests against the inhuman treatment blacks received in the segregated South. These groups were lead by charismatic leaders, in particular SNCC's Stokley Carmichael, who was then a student at Howard University. He would later change his name to Kwame Toure after enlightening sojourns in Africa and embracing the international struggle for human freedom by African people.

Perhaps the most controversial group to emerge from the Black Power movement was the Black Panther Party of self-defense. Founded by Huey P. Newton and Bobby Seale (ironically on my birthday, October 15, 1966), the Panthers launched a crusade for community development and self-protection against a very hostile and violent enemy within the local police departments across America. Historians have always at best misunderstood the Black Panther movement and its significance to the black community's efforts for social equality. They have been depicted as mislead political idealists—or worse, violent subversive communists. What whites do not understand, again due to cognitive dissonance, is that by many political and social standards, the American black community was occupied territory, and they viewed the police as an oppressive military force.

Beginning with slavery, the perpetuated idea was that blacks were animals and had to be contained for the security of the greater white community. This perverted way of thinking continued to the point where numerous innocent unarmed black men in the twentieth century unfairly met their end from white policemen's bullets. To make the unjustified killings worse, the white justice system always acquitted the police, which only served to strengthen the feeling that as victims, the black community needed to evoke their constitutional rights and protect themselves against all aggressors. From the runaway slave who struck the overseer in defiance to the Black Panther party for self-defense, whites, even liberal ones, have always had a problem when black people defended themselves against white oppression. In this case it was the US government and the local police departments. Only when we began to defend our selves against police brutality, lynchings, and racially provoked assaults did the country begin to look inward and debate its moral consciousness concerning its African American population. Sadly history continues to repeat itself; even in the twenty-first century we are dealing with police brutality. All that black people wanted America to do was live up to its ideology of justice and freedom for all, and for the right to compete for fair wages in labor endeavors.

We are presently in the post-civil rights movement, and although significant progress has been made, unfortunately many urban and rural blacks have been left behind. In fact at this time in our history, African Americans have attained greater economic status, greater academic achievements, and stronger representation in the American work force. We even have our first elected African American president. (I will elaborate on this historical occurrence later in the text). However, the opposite side of this paradox is that more black men than ever are incarcerated or in some way caught in the criminal justice system. And as pointed out earlier, in cities such as New York more than 50 percent of black men are unemployed. With the country presently in an economic depression, the unemployed black male statistic has risen to frightening heights.

Drugs and Alcohol

Drugs and alcohol have always played an unwelcomed prominent role in the black community. Unfortunately, many African Americans can attest to the fact that drug abuse and alcoholism has touched their lives in one way or another. Whether it's an immediate family member or a distant cousin, most of us in some way have been affected by these terrible vices.

The criminal justice system, white politicians, and white scholars have long denied America's involvement in the deliberate narcotizing of the black community. The movie *Panther,* by filmmaker Marion Van Peebles, asserts that in the late 1960s, the US government conspired with Latin American drug lords to help flood the urban streets with pure heroin because they feared a black revolution would erupt. With all the other international revolts in Africa and Asia taking place at the time, the United States took certain measures to make sure that the status quo remained undisturbed in this country.

Why is it so difficult for white academia to acknowledge the strong possibility that rather than outright killing black people and subsequently risking world repudiation, the American government realized it was easier to control blacks with illegal drugs. It is a historical fact that in the nineteenth century, when the British invaded China, they colonized them and forced them to become opium addicts. This prompted the Chinese revolution led by Mao Tse Tung, in which the British was successfully kicked out of China. During the Boston tea party, New Englanders didn't want to be taxed without being represented, and they poured the British tea into the Boston harbor, thus launching the Revolutionary War. Likewise, after a century the Chinese refused to be drugged and colonized. However after the Chinese got their independence, the British were able to swindle a hundred-year lease on Hong Kong that just expired in 1998.

In addition to the black community's influx of heroin in the late 1960s, there was the emergence of crack cocaine during the Ronald Reagan presidency of the 1980s. Hundreds of thousands of lives were destroyed during the crack epidemic, including an entire generation of black parents, as the Reagan administration ignored the chaos within the urban black community.

My question to white academia is this: Drugs have always been a cogent and unmessy method to controlling unpopular and undesired segments of society. Why is it unfathomable for people to consider and understand that the US government is a great historian herself and followed the British paradigm to suppress a discontent black community? Even Machiavelli offered this as a means of societal maintenance in his book *The Prince*.

I was born in the 1960s at the height of the black power movement, but I grew up in the seventies, and as a kid I remember seeing dope fiends nodding on the corner. Later on as a teenager in the 1980s, I remember the street violence born out of the crack trade.

How History Affected My Parents

I've always believed that in order to make history relevant, one must connect it directly to one's life. Part of the problem with teaching history to young people is that teachers do so in a manor that gives the perception that students are separate from this history. Specifically, black students would not be sitting in those classrooms if it were not for this history. It is almost as if saying that the civil rights movement occurred, but that was so long ago that it could not possibly have an effect on someone in the twenty-first century. Since the civil rights movement began in the 1960s, only two generations have passed. Therefore the fact that America still suffers psychologically from the disease of racism is evidence that we are still very much connected to this historical time period

My Father

I do not know much about my father's past; he was never one to openly discuss his personal history. He was always very stoic and reticent when my siblings and I posed certain questions about his childhood. It's not as if he would respond sadly or with anger; he would just not say anything, almost as if his brain wanted to recollect and discuss his childhood but could not find the words. I have since concluded that my father must have suffered from some form of social trauma. Compounded with his third grade education, my father perhaps was incapable of recalling anything healthy about growing up in the Jim Crow South.

My father was born around 1934 in Richmond, Virginia. He was one of four brothers. His father died when he was very young, so I can accurately hypothesize that he had no male figure to teach him how to be responsible. He did not realize it then, but he would someday practice that same absence of personal responsibility to his own sons. My father is illiterate, having only gone as far as the third grade. I guess after his father died, he had to abandon his education for the purpose of finding some form of work to help support the family.

My mother told me once that when he was young, perhaps in his early teens, he stole something out of a grocery store. He was caught, and the racist Southern criminal justice system sentenced him to prison with hardened adult male criminals. Bear in mind he was a young teenager, and he spent time on the 'chain gang breaking rocks with a sledgehammer to build a Virginia state highway. It was a harsh penalty for what I'm certain was a petty misdemeanor at best, and I can only speculate as to what psychological scars he bears from being so brutally incarcerated at such a young age. The criminal justice system perpetuates generations of irresponsible men due to its hypocrisy about being fair. However, it is not fair when it comes to black men.

The former New York Supreme Court Justice Bruce Write asserted:

> Today, various studies have found serious inequities in our justice system. One reason, blacks believe, is because those who administer the system of justice are mostly white males. They bring to their professions the same habits of prejudice that are inseparable from the lives they lived, their white neighborhoods, their white clubs and the privileges of a white skin that they have always enjoyed. This is the difficulty in bringing objectivity and impartiality to a jury in a race stricken land. It seems inescapable that white judges reach conclusions that reflect white community standards.

A New Jersey Chief Justice once told me that blacks are more likely to be arrested, less likely to be released on bail, less likely to see members of their own race in the court room and jury box. However they are more likely to be the target of the death penalty hearing when charged with murder, especially if the victim was white.

Pretty much the same conclusion was reached in a 1966 study done by Harry Kalven and Hans Zeisel on the subject of how racist influences affect both judges and jurors in America. It was there demonstrated, if any demonstration was needed, that many jurors refuse to divorce themselves from the racism and prejudice that are a part of their everyday existence.

One white juror, among the many interviewed for the study, put into perspective the general feelings expressed by most, when he spoke of his judgement of a black defendant: "Niggers have to be taught to behave. I feel that if he hadn't done that, he'd probably done something else probably worse and that he should be put away for a good long while.

When I bring up the long history of injustice that blacks have been victimized to my colleagues, they ignore the history and say 'well things are better now'.

With this reference from someone who spent his professional life in the justice system, it is very easy to understand why my father turned out the way he did. Of course there is the concept of personal responsibility and making appropriate choices. However, one must first be exposed to the idea of the personal power they have to control their lives. According to Nathaniel Branden's paradigm of self, due to his environmental circumstances my father subconsciously felt that his life choices were limited because of his race, and it was difficult for him to envision a more positive future for himself.

The idea of improving self-esteem only works when we are taught about decision making, taking personal responsibility, and avoiding scapegoat thinking. This way of thinking does not arrive in a vacuum. On top of collaboration with a hostile, racist environment, if your parents had no idea what self-esteem was, how could they possibly teach it to their children? It is very difficult to teach what we don't know.

With no education and the experience of prison as a child-raising tool, my father only learned how to become a hustler. This was his livelihood and his psychosocial mode of survival in the highly competitive world of hustlers, which is all too common within the urban environment. My father was very successful at hustling, and while growing up I can remember him dressed sharply and always having a wad of cash. He also owned and drove around in fancy cars. Although I never saw this, I was informed by my mother that he would freely fool around with other women in the community while she always had to struggle to get any kind of money out of him to care for her children. My father would come to the house periodically. and he and my mother would always end up in a fight about his blatant disregard concerning his parental responsibilities.

Incidentally, my father would always pick on my oldest brother, who was not his biological son. My brother began exhibiting homosexual tendencies early on, and my father, drunk on alcohol, would tease him. They would end up in heated arguments and sometimes fight. However, the interesting thing about that was after cursing my father out earlier in the day, my mother would always take my father's side against my brother. It was clear even then that my mother suffered from low self-esteem, and this dictated her decisions regarding her priorities.

The seventies came to an end, and my father's illustrious career as a hustler started to wane. Due to poor planning and no foresight for the future, his game started to slip. During the eighties he no longer drove the fancy cars and was barely able to hustle enough money to feed himself. There are no retirement funds or 401Ks for aging hustlers. All of his nice clothes were gone, replaced by faded dungarees, tattered shoes, and rumpled shirts. He was no longer the top dog in the streets. Time eventually replaced him with younger, hungrier, and more violent hustlers due to the crack epidemic in the black community. He was always a heavy drinker, but his alcohol intake severely increased during this time. He had no interest in getting substance abuse treatment, and I suspect that on some level he recognized his epoch was over and tried to dull the reality of him becoming a vagabond.

During the nineties, after getting arrested for soliciting marijuana, my father returned back to his hometown of Richmond, Virginia. He was staying with his firstborn daughter, but his heavy drinking quickly wore out his welcome by becoming more of a burden. She asked him to leave, and he returned to Boston for a short time.

The last time I saw my father was in February 1999. I was in Boston visiting my mother, and he happened to be in town as well. Against my personal wishes, my mother contacted him, and he came by. The encounter was an emotional experience for me, and I asked him how could his conscience allowed him to live with himself after being such an irresponsible parent. He simply responded, "Nobody's perfect," as if that fully explained his unwillingness toward his parental obligations. He never apologized, and with the life he chose to lead, ironically at his old age he began to scapegoat white society for his shortcomings. I vehemently disagreed with him because although I knew the sociological, historical, and political circumstances under which he was born into, he still had the power of personal choice. Racism is a reason, but it should not be an excuse for failure; it should be used as motivation to aspire to succeed.

I can honestly say that at the time of this writing, I have no knowledge of his whereabouts. I believe my mother maintains occasional communication with him, however I presently have no overwhelming desire to speak with him. I am prepared to live out the rest of my life fully cognizant of the consequences of this decision.

My Mother

I explained how oppressive Jim Crow racism affected my father's self-esteem and influenced his decisions as he grew into adulthood. My mother was affected by Northern racism as opposed to Southern racism, and her story is different.

My mother was born during Jim Crow in 1946 in Goldsboro, North Carolina. She told me she was not raised by my grandmother in her earlier years and instead was raised by her aunt. She later moved to Harlem, New York, with her father and spent her adolescent years there. Finally she moved to Boston when she was around twelve or thirteen years old, to live with her mother.

My mother was a victim of her time in terms of not being able to recognize how certain cultural traditions go unquestioned and can possibly be a detriment to one's self-esteem. As mentioned earlier, the black community is notoriously unforgiving against cultural deviance, such as homosexuality, substance abuse, mental illness, and teenage pregnancy. However, the hypocrisy of this is a thick shroud of secrecy that envelops a family when the issue of incest and child molestation becomes apparent. Often the mother of the daughter is in denial and does not want to accept that it is happening.

In those days the family would be more concerned about the stigma from shame that the offending family member put on them and they would take measures to banish the child to mental institutions or, if they could afford it, an in-patient drug treatment program. They would hide the daughter's pregnancy by sending her "down South" to be with grandparents. If a male family member was homosexual, he would be ostracized. With molestation, unfortunately the victim was usually perceived as the encourager of the crime

My mother never elaborated about her experiences growing up with my grandmother. However, I know that at times there was turmoil between her and her other siblings. As a young girl, my mother had been molested by an older relative and probably felt that she could not report this to her mother. Due to the black community's unwillingness to address embarrassing problems for fear of airing the family's dirty laundry, perhaps she felt she couldn't go to my grandmother. Or perhaps she did disclose it to her but did not receive the appropriate level of support she deserved. I'm sure this explains her ambiguity toward my grandmother in her teenage and early adult years. As a victim of such a heinous crime, this had a profound effect of her self-esteem and subsequently influenced the decisions she would make in the future.

In retrospect I can see that as a result of that criminal act, my mother's self-esteem was significantly lower than my father's was. Her poor self-esteem is on a deeper subconscious level of hatred for being born black in a society that deprecates black people. Although she never was involved in drugs or alcohol abuse, she still made several poor life decisions as a result of not fully learning to love who she was and embrace being born black. It seemed at times that she felt being black was a punishment or a cruel joke played on her by nature. She admired white people but also feared them and how much power they wielded in society. My mother is a very intelligent woman, however due to her self-esteem issues, she never actualized her full potential.

My mother was the oldest of nine children, five of which were born contemporarily with me and my brothers. As of today three of my mother's siblings have died before their times from problems related to drugs. Uncle Raymond died from a heroin overdose in 1977. Aunt Denise, who struggled with a lifelong addiction to heroin, died from drug-related health problems in 1993. Uncle Mark, like my brother Glenn, was diagnosed with HIV and died in 2005 from health complications; he was also entangled with an addiction to cocaine before he passed away.

My mother never fully got along with her siblings; throughout the years I've been alive, she has always maintained an erratic and sometimes volatile relationship with them. Due to her low self-esteem, she never fully understood the idea of not worrying about what others do. She always saw herself as a victim in one way or another. She had a manifestation of being victimized and a feeling that someday someone would come to her rescue her from undesirable circumstances.

My mother always based her relationships on how someone treated her. At this time it is fair to say that no one taught her the principle of personal accountability, because apparently my grandmother did not know it either. Subsequently, my mother spent her life reacting to people; she was always preoccupied with what someone said about her, what someone did to her, and how someone thought about her. This obsession is a strong, symptomatic response to low self-esteem, which she unfortunately passed down to my brothers and myself.

My mother became pregnant and gave birth to my oldest ⋅ when she was just sixteen years old. She never school, and under the circumstances she was forced to enter the workforce, starting with the post office, after my youngest brother was born in 1968.

I never met Glen's father, however like my father he was irresponsible as a parent. My mothers' low self-esteem led her to make terrible decisions regarding male companionship. According to her, she met my father through a friend, and I was born approximately a year later. Evaluating a potential partner is definitely influenced by one's self-esteem. My mother knew my father was a hustler when she met him. She knew he did not work for a living and was uneducated. She knew he was married but estranged from his wife in Virginia. Nonetheless, she made the choice to allow him to become the father of her last two sons.

In a rational world where people take responsibility for their decisions, my mother should not have been surprised when my father failed to comply with his parental obligations. Based on my father's profile, she should have seen it coming. She did not and was perhaps in some form of denial herself, thus beginning many years of conflict, and sometime violent encounters, with him.

I was born at the height of the civil rights movement and Black Power in this country, however my mother chose not to be a part of this dynamic era, and she did not take advantage of the opportunities that were opening up for black people at this time. She was shortsighted after being fired from the post office, and she did not return to work but instead embarked on her own hustling career. This included credit card scams and several other ways to ascertain money to support a good lifestyle. To this day

I'm still in the dark regarding everything that my mother did.

Consistent with the urban value system of materialism, my mother sported a very fine wardrobe that gave the appearance she was doing well. However with no job, no financial help from her children's fathers, and the unpredictability of success from one hustle to the next, there were many times when life was very difficult.

My mother wanted to be middle-class even if it meant living beyond her means. This is difficult to attain when the only consistent form of income is a monthly welfare check. In those days welfare was designed to help underprivileged people meet the necessities of daily living. There were a lot of good social programs that included being able to go to college while on welfare. Presidents Linden B. Johnson, Gerald Ford, and Jimmy Carter attempted to address some of the inequalities of the black community by offering special social assistance to struggling families. Due to my mother's detrimental value system and low self-esteem, she did not take advantage of any of them. When Ronald Reagan came into office in the eighties, he cut those programs, and I remember my family suffering through some of our worst economic times during his first term in office.

I remember one time period in which things were so bad economically that it ate at the very fabric of our emotional well-being. I was in the eighth grade, and perhaps due to some bureaucratic mix-up, the welfare check was about two or three months late. My mother was on the phone daily trying to convince these people to send some money for her struggling family. I guess part of the problem was the welfare saw through some systematic scam she had been trying to run and temporary cut off the benefits. Finally one day a retroactive check came in the mail for over a thousand dollars. My mother, my brothers, and I were so happy that we were on the brink of tears.

The early 1980s were a challenging period for me. In middle school I remembered always being depressed and making a vain attempt at suicide. I swallowed a bottle of Tylenol tablets and told my mother what I had done. She called poison control, and they said that because I was young and healthy, the Tylenol would not adversely affect me. I realize now that it was an aggressive cry for my mother's attention. During my early years growing up, my mother gave what I call obligatory attention to her children. Her self-esteem was so bad that she would often scapegoat her children as the cause of her misfortunes in life, and at times she would tell us so. This hurt us a great deal, and I carried this well into my adult hood. As a family unit, even under the most difficult of financial circumstances, children should feel a sense of being loved from their parents. I can honestly say that I did not feel loved by my mother growing up. She would say she loved me, and in her own way I'm certain that she did, however I never felt it.

Although my mother did not abuse drugs or alcohol, due to her weak self-esteem and her irresponsible concept of what a parent should be, oftentimes it felt as though we were living with a parent with a substance abuse problem. All of the eccentric behaviors were there—blaming of others for her problem, being unwilling to work, attaining money through deviant behavioral means that would compromise her integrity, and having an occasional violent tendency toward her children when we did not act well or questioned her behavior. As a result of all of this, I grew to hate my mother intensely. I blamed her for the reason why we were a poor and fragmented family. My anger toward her had nothing to do with any particular love for my father. I did not long after him, and because he was such an inconsistent factor in my life, it felt natural when he was not around and unnatural when he was. I blamed my mother for being unwilling to work and begin the responsible endeavor of appropriately taking care of her family. To my peers we were embarrassingly poor.

Allow me to impart my opinion on being in poverty: Being poor hurts your self-esteem and your subjective reality on various levels. Being poor affects you emotionally, psychologically, intellectually, socially, behaviorally, and on a grander scale politically. You have virtually no power as an individual when you are poor. I hated being poor because it made me hate myself and implied that my existence was an accident. As a young black male, it made me think that something was wrong with me and confirmed that the white race was superior.

As I started to learn and understand the concept of self-esteem, I realized that my mother's level of self-love was so low that she could not possibly give unconditional love to anyone because she did not love herself. As a result of my personal self-healing, I learned to forgive her for all the emotional pain and suffering I felt that she caused. I learned that she was operating from an inadequate formula on how to address life herself, and subsequently she was ill equipped to handle many of life's challenges.

A large part of my mother's inability to deal with life's pressures was her obvious desire to be in a functional relationship with a man. As mentioned earlier, my mother came from an era that upheld the religious and cultural beliefs that men were the masters of women in the eyes of God. My mother's self-esteem was never strong enough for her to stand emotionally independent. She always saw her value within the context of being with a man.

Starting with Glen's father, my mother subconsciously embarked on a lifelong struggle of consistently choosing negative men as potential mates or partners. These men had their own self-esteem issues and were not positive contributors to society. They were all unemployed uneducated hustlers. She once mentioned to me that when she met my father, she saw him as a father figure because of the absence of her father in her life. She never realized or fully understood that her choice in men was a direct reflection on how she valued herself.

My mother's self-esteem was at a sufficient level that she could function in society and even compile a few achievements, such as always having a roof over our heads and owning several cars. However, she was always happiest when she had a man in her life.

The interesting thing is that to this day my mother honestly believes that her behavior while we were younger should not have had a negative impact on our emotional well-being. However, her behavior had an enormous impact on how I viewed myself. I know that my low self-esteem had a direct connection to her irresponsible behavior as a parent. Due to her poor lever of self-esteem, my mother was never fully able to take responsibility for her actions. In fact, my mother always maintained a thick layer of denial regarding herself and her decision too not fully return to the work force.

Followed by the success of the civil rights movement in the sixties, the seventies ushered in the Women's Liberation Movement along with a significant number of new opportunities that were not openly available to women in the past.

In *Strangers to These Shores,* Vincent Parrillo states, "The 1960s was a decade of social activism inspired by many factors, including President Kennedy's appointment of a Presidential commission on the status of women, whitish documented extensive sexual discrimination in the country. When Congress failed to act on the commission's recommendation's a number of feminist advocates formed the National Organization for Women (NOW), in 1966, and a new phase of the feminist movement began. Resisted at first by most other women's groups, the new left, and even civil-rights group, the women's liberation movement eventually gained acceptance, succeeding in its efforts to end many forms of sex discrimination, particularly economic ones."

As with the Black Power Movement, my mother chose not to recognize the Women's Liberation Movement at this time, and Parrillo's text provides a sufficient answer as to why. "Low income African American women did not identify with the feminist movement because many of its demands then seemed irrelevant to their needs."

African American feminist Bell Hooks observed, "Today's masses of Black women in the US refuse to acknowledge that they have much to gain by the feminist struggle. They fear feminism. They have stood in place so long that they are afraid to move. They fear change. The fear losing what little they have. They are afraid to openly confront white feminists with their racism or Black males with their sexism, not to mention white males with their racism and sexism." I concur with this assertion, and in the case of my mother, she definitely fit within this sociological paradigm.

Nonetheless, it would be unfair of me to not to mention the many great things my mother did for me. She was very instrumental in my pursuit of a college education. In 1987 after I turned my life around, I was preparing to attend St. Augustine's college in Raleigh, North Carolina. About a week before I was to register for classes, I spoke with the college rep from the bursar's office. She informed me that I would need two thousand dollars cash to enroll for the semester. I worked that summer to raise money for school, however I had nothing close to that kind of money. When I revealed this to my mother, she became angry and rightfully chastised me for my irresponsibility in not better preparing for the situation.

I was depressed, thinking that I had blown my opportunity to go away for college. Then on the day before I was scheduled to leave for North Carolina, my mother handed me more than two thousand dollars cash. Subsequently, I was able to register for my first semester at St. Augustine.

That was not the first time my mother came through for me, and I acknowledge that she played a significant role in my academic success. Nonetheless, I wish her self-esteem had been stronger back then, which would have allowed her to make better decisions and reach her full potential.

I also realize that because I went to college, I had the opportunity to have great experiences and come in contact with positive people. These great mentors and role models—Tony Williams at Brandies University; Dr. Kamau Kambon at St. Augustine; Professor Jaworski at Fairley Dickerson University; Dr. Barbara Wheeler, Dr. Donald Wheeler, and Prof. James Conyers at Kean University; Professors John Errinberg and Patrice McSherry at Long Island University—had a hand in furthering my development as a human being. My educational experiences also put me on the path to having an open mind that allowed me to be receptive to learning new ideas such as how having a healthy self-esteem level can improve the quality of life.

My mother did not go to college and did not have positive experiences with many of the people she encountered throughout her life. Because of this she developed an intense distrust and dislike of black people—and subsequently herself. Vincent Parrillo describes this concept of negative self-image as "the result of social conditioning differential treatment, or both causing people or groups to believe themselves inferior." This definition certainly explains a great deal about my mother's idiosyncrasies, her value system, and her decision making process throughout her life.

Several changes have occurred in my mother's life since my brother died. Up until that point he was the only one left in the house providing company for her; my brothers Parrish and I had moved away years earlier. When Glen died, she was left alone in Boston and experienced some difficult economic times, moving twice in three years this. However her housing circumstances appear to be stable at this point. The prevailing issue now is her own failing health. Along with her other ailments, decades of cigarette smoking has finally caught up with her. She complains of always being weak and feeling tired. At fifty-nine, her health is not going to improve overnight, especially when she still is in denial about the detrimental effects of her continued smoking. Nonetheless, she is my mother, and I love her very much. I just wish she'd actively pursued self-esteem enhancement so that her life could have been happier.

This book is about having and attaining self-love. In essence I realize that my mother is the victim of a larger machination called the ideology of white supremacy. With no strong past family frame of reference, no adequate economic or social support system, no clear sense of who she was, no historical connection, and no self-love self-esteem, she became what the majority culture expected her to become: an unwed, unemployed black mother of three who abused the public assistance system. My mother did not understand that she could have made different choices and perhaps lived a different life due to her limited scope and the social frame of reference in her thinking.

My relationship with my mother has improved over the years. I speak to her once a week and have since developed a new love for her. In many respects I have no idea of the emotional and psychological pain and suffering she had to endure while trying to raise three snotty-nosed boys by herself. When I step outside myself and look at the situation from her perspective, given her poor self-esteem and those weak social and economic conditions, it was very difficult to make any other type of life decisions. Based on this understanding, I have since learned to forgive her.

Chapter 3
Accepting Ourselves as Black People

It is very difficult to have dark skin in a world that seemingly only values white or light skin. From birth human beings are inculcated with the image that white is the color of beauty, purity, preference, and privilege. People are further programmed with this image through Christianity and other media, such as Michelangelo's depiction of Jesus Christ in his Renaissance paintings.

It is taboo to discuss this in our community, however our self-hate runs so deep that the very genetic characteristics that make us people of African descent is so deeply deprecated that black people will look to have children with white people for the purpose of having a lighter-skinned babies. The rationalization is that perhaps these children will have better opportunities in life than their black parent.

This is evident throughout Latin America, in which over time the former slaves of a once black race has become genetically lighter over the generations. Due to their profound socialization of a negative-self image, whether subconsciously or consciously, they have created a race that is more acceptable to the standard of appearance for the white race.

In *Strangers to These Shores,* Vincent Parrillo states,

> "Continual treatment as an inferior encourages a loss of self-confidence. If everything about a person's position and experiences-jobs with low pay, substandard housing, the hostility of others, and the need for assistance from government agencies, works to destroy pride and hope, the person may become apathetic.

> The pervasiveness of dominant-group values and attitudes, which include negative stereotypes of the minority group, may cause the minority group to absorb them. A person's self image includes race religion and nationality; thus, individuals may feel embarrassed, even inferior, if they see that one or more of the attributes they posses are despised within the society. In effect, minority group members began to perceive themselves as negatively as the dominant group originally did".

When we look at black people in the context of not accepting themselves, there is a four-hundred-year history of detrimental socialization that helped facilitate this phenomenon. As mentioned earlier in this text, black people in this country are different from any other ethnic group. From our history to our appearance, we have been treated with such inequality and enmity, and over time this has had a self-deprecating effect on us as a group. Due to easily identifiable characteristics such as darker skin color, thicker hair texture, and stronger facial features, we stand out prominently in a society that recognizes white skin, straight hair texture, and softer facial features.

During earlier colonial America, men and women from Africa and England both arrived in the colony for the same purpose. The goal was to attain sponsorship from a rich colonist and negotiate payment for passage to the colony. In return, the servant would perform labor duties for the colonist for an agreed amount of time, bound by contract. When the contract expired and the debt was successfully repaid, the newly freed servant was to receive a small plaque of land along with livestock and a mule to help initiate his new autonomous life as a pioneer. However as evidenced through writing from colonial times, whereas whites were viewed as servants, blacks were almost always viewed differently. Because of their physical differences, they were viewed as slaves and treated accordingly.

In *A People's History of the United States,* Howard Zinn points out some of those differences. Zinn retraces a 1639-40 legal decree that illustrates all persons except those of negro descent were to receive arms and ammunition. In addition Zinn explains that in 1640, three servants tried to escape from their plantation and master, two whites and one black African. They were apprehended, and the two whites were punished with a simple lengthening of their service to their master. The punishment for the African, however, was to "serve his master for the rest of his natural born life."

From one of the earliest slave-master accounts in American history, we can derive where this socialization of an inferiority complex was first instilled in black people, and we can follow its progress: the first servants in the seventeenth century, the official legalization and economic practice of slavery, the Jim Crow era in which preferential racial segregation dictated the quality of one's life, the twenty-first-century post-civil rights world in which there are still very few positive depictions of black people. Today the image of a black man still conjures up emotions of hate, fear, and derision in other members of American society.

Blacks are at a profound psychological disadvantage of trying to find self-love within the sociological parameters of Americanism. Unfortunately, many of us are born and raised in this world in a maternal, single-headed household. Our fathers are not present, and we are brought up in very economically and socially challenging environments that are oftentimes very violent. Because of those conditions, we adopt a certain value system of survival based on the rules of these neighborhoods. We attend public schools that are woefully inadequate in providing the appropriate educational services and self-esteem enhancements our special needs sometimes warrant.

This inept education masquerades itself as a sufficient vehicle to prepare a people over the next twelve years of their lives. In reality the education system and many of its players only serve to maintain society's status quo by ill preparing a segment of society in their efforts to compete with the larger society. Since the institutions themselves reflect the American culture of dislike of black people, they subsequently succeed in reinforcing detrimental stereotypes and inculcating the foundation of poor self-esteem.

Finally, combine this with an overwhelming economic and political social media engine that empowers the members of the majority white American culture by continual reinforcement of images of what's considered beautiful, successful, pure, virtuous, hardworking, preferred, and acceptable. These are powerful messages sent by the machinations of American society through various media forms, and depending on one's race and ethnicity, it can have a strong influence in determining the outcome of someone's life. *CBS Nightline* conducted a study on stereotypes on students from various universities. The study discovered interesting results about how people are trained to think about themselves and others. The study supports this assertion that blacks are still veiwed less positively when comparedto other races. Based on this study, it is no wonder why it is so difficult to be black in America. Through social conditioning, the entire society has been trained to dislike, distrust, and reject the black race. Juxtaposed with the lack of political, economic, and social power, the victims of this broad form of discrimination suffer from the syndrome of a negative self-image.

In addition, in the August 2007 edition of *Ebony* magazine, there is an article titled "I Am Not White" that features blacks that are so light that they are successful in passing for white in America. The article discusses the lives of five people of African American heritage and their experiences regarding their appearances. In most circles, it was believed that their white skin complexion and straight hair texture gave them an advantage in American society that allowed them to take advantage of the educational and economic resources available. "Racism and colorism is still an issue, declared Sandra E. Taylor, professor of sociology at Clark Atlanta University and states that studies have indicated that beauty and power are closely correlated to lighter skin in America".

In every interviewee's personal account across several decades, while passing for white in white social circles, they have heard casual racist comments aimed against black people. In some cases their dilemma was one of telling white people that they are black and facing the consequences, or simply continuing to pass.

What I found most intriguing was the case in which one of the interviewee's relatives completely repudiates her African's ancestry and passes for white by wearing blue contacts and dying her hair blonde; she disappeared into the white world. never to be seen again by her family. It is also fair to mention that they explained how they also have faced prejudice within the black community. Because of their features, the black community penalized them for not being "black enough."

In *Maximum Self-Esteem,* Jerry Minchinton asserts that "as far as personal worth is concerned, absolutely nothing sets us apart from anyone else. None of these complaints about ourselves make us better or more important. In the case of blacks, more so than anyone else, it just make us different. There is no criteria to measure individual worth." As descendents of the African race, we sometimes live in a very difficult social reality. It is imperative that we accept ourselves unconditionally. With the exception of Michael Jackson, the abundant reality is our physical appearance is not going to change. Based on this fact, it is mentally healthier to learn to unconditionally love who we are and use this energy to improve the quality of our lives. We are born with certain gifts and deficiencies that nature engineered for every member of the human race. Hence, no race is biologically superior or inferior to any other. As black people, we need to learn to celebrate being different.

According to Minchinton, "as far as personal worth is concerned, absolutely nothing sets us apart from anyone else. There are no criteria by which to measure individual worth. We have no need or obligation to prove our worth to anyone, including our selves; our existence alone is sufficient evidence."

Branden elaborates a bit further when he provides three levels of self-acceptance. The first level states, "to be self accepting is to be on my own side and to be for my self. Self-acceptance is the value and commitment that derives from the fact that I am alive and conscious. As such, it is more primitive than self-esteem. It is a prerational, premoral act of self-affirmation. This is a kind of natural egoism that is the birthright of every human being." By "to be on my own side," he means you should act, think, and behave in a self-aware manner. Your everyday consciousness and decision making is directed toward self-enhancement in the various aspects of your life. Acknowledge that you are alive and healthy, that you have a natural birthright to exist. Despite the negative concepts regarding egoism, a basic level of egoism is needed to function in life. Furthermore, "to be on my own side" does not mean to be egotistical or selfish; it simply refers to the fact that you have a right to accept yourself as you are.

Brandon's second level is "our willingness to experience and accept that we think what we think, feel what we feel, desire what we desire, have done what we have done and are what we are . . . It is the our willingness to experience rather than to disown whatever may be the facts of our being at a particular moment. To think our thoughts, own our feelings, be present to the reality of our behavior. I interpret this to mean to respect and appreciate your own thoughts feelings and opinions, even if they are counter to a popular notion. Due to the profound hegemony of the American white capitalistic way of thinking, the pressure to streamline one's opinions is enormous. It becomes easier to be nonobjective and have our opinions congruent with mainstream America, even against our better judgment. This is a very important piece to the self-esteem puzzle. In all fairness, one of the unique qualities that sets America apart from past civilizations is the promotion of individual thought and the development of the independent self. This powerful idea, combined with a different political and economic vision, helped catapult the United States into the most successful former colony of Great Britain and established the paradigm that other newly independent countries followed.

Over the last 250 years, the ideological, political, and economic practices have become flexible to meet the contemporary needs of each new American generation. Nonetheless, the basic principle of the individual and the development of self still remain.

Due to the hegemonic white American value system, the political and economic conditions of any given times, and the international conflicts that direly involve the United

States, it becomes difficult to assert a contrary opinion without being labeled unpatriotic or anti-American.

The United States is in a war with Iraq that continues to be a long and tiresome waste of political and military engagement. Many black politicians, corporate and legal leaders, and average working-class citizens do not agree with the war. Subsequently, when we give our opinions, especially in a broad media form, the propaganda machine of the current political administration criticizes us and looks to sanction those opposing voices.

As black people in America, we have almost always held contradictory opinions to any military conflict with which America is connected. From the Revolutionary War in which black slave wanted the British to win, to the war for the Philippines in the early twentieth century in which black soldiers defected and fought against the colonizing of the Philippines, to Dr. Martin Luther King's repudiation of the Vietnam War—the difference in ideas is usually contingent on the individual's or the group's frame of reference. Because African Americans have had different experiences than other groups within the scope of Americanism, in most cases the outlook of our geopolitical opinions are different from the mainstream because of how we have been treated in the historical context.

Brandon's explanation of the second level is particularly applicable because as human beings, we do have a right to think, feel, experience, desire, and express what we want. It is our god-given right to do this. Until recently, the majority of American culture has been successful in writing us out of world and American history. In addition, when the conversation of race and inequality comes up, they do not want us to discuss slavery or long-term discriminatory practices aimed exclusively at the black race. The majority culture will give examples of other ethnic groups and how they have been successful in attaining the American dream. As an African American with some academic credentials, I know that the pathology of other ethnic groups was and still is significantly different from the African American. Therefore, we have a right to own our history, opinions, feelings, and experiences, and we should defend them with historical accuracy.

Brandon's third level is, "Self-acceptance entails the idea of compassion, of being a friend to myself . . . Self-acceptance has a compassionate interest that does not encourage undesirable behavior but reduces the likelihood of it recurring." This suggests that we need to actively practice the art of accepting ourselves as we are, faults and all.

Poor levels of self-esteem allow individuals to remain in an insecure, depressing, self-hating state. With such a weak outlook on life and why they do the things they do, the poor decision making has a strong likelihood of continuing. When we are emotional, whether it's extended periods of anger or sadness, we usually make poor decisions. This is because our emotions block any attempt at reasonable thought to see the problem issue in its entirety. We are not asking ourselves where did this come from or what prompted this behavior.

Healthy self-esteem acknowledges the thought and the act, takes responsibility for the behavior, and more important forgives the self. Strong self-esteem will make one ask, "Why did I do that?" and introspectively seek to understand the decision that led to the behavior. After the internal cleaning has been initiated, strong self-esteem lets one live more consciously about the mundane decision making within everyday life. With such consciousness, the likelihood of the deprecated behavior decreases because the reasoning behind evaluating the pros and cons of decisions provides a crystal ball as to what is the most likely outcome. From there it can be determined if this is a desirable course of action to take. In most cases, we can make the appropriate decision and subsequently be at peace with the outcome, thus reducing the likelihood of repeated detrimental behavior.

As black Americans, unfortunately a great deal of the actions in our community give rise to the speculation that historically, we have had a problem accepting ourselves. Again, due to the fact that we are so radically different in appearance from the white norm, some black people in this country are socialized from birth into a condition of ineptness and inferiority. More specifically, when we derive from the worst neighborhoods in a particular city—and some cases the gripping reality is that of poverty, welfare, substance abuse, and violence—we mentally absorb this image and conform to it.

In my several years of service to the black community as a case manager and vocational trainer, I have encountered individuals that spent most of most of their lives struggling with substance abuse and conforming to the idea that violence solves personal problems.

The black community has its own rules and concepts on norms. However plenty of these codes are detrimental to its inhabitants. I have met younger and older black men who told me that they tried crack or heroin because of peer pressure. In most cases it was because they grew up watching their parents' illicit substance abuse, and this was the only frame of reference of life they had. Likewise violence, which has always been an integral part of the black community, is the only means to settle disputes because this is what people see on a continual basis.

I remember once I was running a violence reduction group for one of the many programs for which I worked, and the question was posed about what to do in a if one is confronted with a potentially violent situation. It is necessary that I elaborate a little further about the population I held in audience: a group of recovering addicts and ex convicts from Brownsville Brooklyn, widely recognized as one of the most dangerous neighborhoods in New York City. I suggested to them that if they were confronted with violence such as and armed robbery attempt, give up their possessions and call the police. My solution was met with laughter, with one woman commenting, "What grown man is going to run to the police for help? He'd better fight for his shit!"

I remember choosing my words very carefully. I explained, "A man is no good to his family dead or in jail. In neither case are you able to provide anything for your family. Therefore what is the purpose of acting resistant in the scope of potential mortal danger, when it is a high plausibility that you will be imprisoned for the rest of your life—or no longer alive to boast about it? Each time you wake is another opportunity to change the direction of your life, to learn new ideas and break negative behavioral patterns. This is the real legacy you leave for your family, to persevere against formidable odds." Unfortunately, my scenario prove to be prophetic: one of the young men from that program was murdered a few weeks later in a mugging attempt, and he resisted. He left behind two young sons.

I pose this to suggest that this is the psychological and social behavior of a community that refuses to accept itself. The unstated feeling is that being born black in America is a sentence to a lifetime of poverty, suffering, and an untimely death.

However, with the principles of self-acceptance used to bolster ones self-esteem level, one can significantly reduce the likelihood of making certain negative decisions that lead to violent outcomes. It does not matter that an individual was born in Brownsville; by unconditionally accepting and loving that we are black and a member of the human race, we move onto a road of wiser decision making that reduces the probability of violence and increases the chances of success.

Chapter Four

Taking Responsibility for Our Behavior as Black People

I have always understood that social practices and personal responses to environmental stimuli are socialized, learned behavior. I believe that if a person is not able, under any given circumstance, to assert her ability to address the various issues in her life, it is because she received poor responsibility training from her parents. I realize that the outcome of this assertion is buried in statistics in which numerous individuals developed into incredibly responsible people despite having parents who fell short of being responsible. In many cases I have met individuals who were raised under less than desirable conditions and still persevered by taking responsibility for the outcome of their lives. However greater numbers of statistics suggest that children often pick up and carry on the negative behaviors of their parents, primarily because the home is the first essential socialization tool to convey any given value system. This is the most significant frame of reference through which children are socialized in order to learn how to address life's problems. If the parents do not have effective coping tools to handle the pressures of child rearing, employment commitments, and socially appropriate adult interactions, then in most cases this behavior is past down to their children. This helps explain the continued generations of uneducated, unemployed, violence prone, and substance abusing blacks.

If someone is raised in a home environment in which

- parents do not value work and are subsidized by public assistance;
- parents unabashedly abuse drugs and alcohol in the presence of their children;
- fathers completely abandoned their children or at best played a marginal role in their lives;
- parents behave sexually inappropriately in the presence of children; and/or
- parents are generally unaware that they are teaching a detrimental value system to their children,

unfortunately in most cases these children will grow up to replicate the behavior they learned from their parents.

The irresponsible behavior of the American black family has roots that date back at least three generations. During the Jim Crow era, life was a very difficult for American blacks. The goal was to maintain the Southern status quo and keep the American black disenfranchised. Most often Jim Crow laws were enforced though some of the most outstanding acts of violence aimed toward subjugating black people. In addition, the violence was legal and socially acceptable because the Southern white power structure felt that it was necessary to ensure the supremacy of the white race. Although not as violent, the North instituted similar discriminatory social codes that were very effective in keeping social distance between whites and blacks.

Parrillo describes the emergence of Jim Crow as "A cultural drift that change people's values. Economic problems, scandals and frustrations endured by southern whites helped to foster this cultural shift. In a region where they had long been considered inferior, many Blacks were achieving socioeconomic respectability and becoming economic competitors. Resentment at Black upward mobility, amplified by a historical undercurrent of racist attitudes, was further increased by economic troubles such as declining cotton prices and unemployment. Because blacks were racially distinct, they became a convenient scapegoat for the frustrations and hostility of southern whites."

Slavery was a crime and an absolute travesty against another member of the human race. Nonetheless, through intense study and research I have concluded that after emancipation in 1865, the successive eighty-plus years of practiced legal apartheid in the form of Jim Crow was the most dangerous and most psychologically damaging to the African American. The crimes against the black race that took place during this time period was responsible for economical and social lag with which those future generations of blacks were forced to deal.

In order to foster healthy self-esteem, one must create and nurture a sense of identity and purpose. During slavery this was not possible because we were stolen from our African homeland and coerced by the ever-present threat of violence to perform our labor duties for the economic benefit of our masters. It was not a reality to continue the practice of our African cultures and customs because we had been socialized to forget and abandon our indigenous selves and accept being chattel labor as a form of survival. However, after multiple generations of labor work, we mastered relevant agriculture, carpentry, and other vocational trades that would prove invaluable to our economic livelihood and our upward mobility after slavery ended. Former slaves were able to attain work and gain an economic presence primarily because we could do the work in a more cost-effective way than the native white Southerners or the other newly arrived ethnic groups.

Black colleges surfaced with the promise of higher learning, and with this upsurge in social economic mobility, American blacks began to experience early forms of a healthy self-esteem as they accepted their sense of purpose and conformed to their roles as family members and economic providers. This opened the door to a new sense of identity—not necessarily as an African but as an American African from which they drew family values, cultural pride, and a standard of excellence from.

But in a series of events that was fueled by frightened whites who created political, social. and economic changes, that new sense of self-esteem and indigenous American black identity was severely compromised for the next generations to come. From the late 1890s to the mid-1960s, approximately five generations of American blacks were adversely affected by the Jim Crow segregation of the South and the accepted social segregation of the North. Black men and women lived with domestic terrorism day in and day out. This experience had a profound effect on the collective mental stability and outlook of the black community.

One of the defination of the word "responsible" means to have the ability to respond, or be able to respond. Arguably this is more easily accomplished when one has strong self-esteem, a sense of identity, and a sense of purpose. Combined with social and economic resources, a person not only will experience a sense of identity and purpose and improved self-esteem, it also increases the person's ability to respond i.e. to be responsible.

In the 1950s blacks were still barred from attending the best universities in America despite the display of their intellectual capabilities. They were the last ones hired at most jobs, paid the least for doing the same amount or more work than white counterparts, fired first, and openly discriminated against. In general they lived in the worst section of any city, county, or town. Local—and state-elected officials often neglected the infrastructures of black communities, whether they were Democrat or Republican. At any given time a black man could face the possibility of being the victim of random violence from rogue white supremacist groups such as the Ku Klux Klan—and his surviving family would not be vindicated in any court of law. A black woman could be raped and bear the children of her rapist but not receive any restitution for the criminal act committed against her.

As a result of these terrorist tactics, American blacks were forced back into the social mode of acceptance, which Parrillo defines as a "minority groups response to prejudice and discrimination based on powerlessness, fear for personal safety, desires for economic security or fatalism." My theory is that under these conditions, despite the resiliency of many of their community members, blacks' collective sense of responsibility or ability to respond had waned in the face of a reality that inculcates an inferiority complex within black people: A father who possesses a low level of education and can only attain physical labor type employment. A son who grew up seeing his father become increasingly frustrated because he could not find work that paid sufficiently to support his family. A father during the Jim Crow years who is virtually powerless to assert any authority or even protect his family. A father that feels mentally castrated because of the brutal racism he faces daily. A son who watches his father self-medicate with alcohol and becomes reticent and bitter toward himself and life to the point where he gives up and emotionally or, in many cases, physically abandons the family.

The son perpetuates this reaction to the challenges of life as he also views substance abuse, destructive vices, and abandonment as a viable solution to his own problems with his family and life. The subconscious choice to be irresponsible comes as a natural reaction and subsequently fosters a multigenerational social phenomenon because there was never really an appropriate frame of reference to teach a young person how to become a responsible adult.

A social explanation as to why white people have attained and maintained middle class status is first that they had a 150-year head start in terms of economic and social stability; they did not have laws or special rules that impeded their progress toward economic stability. Second, in most cases the parents are married, which is a vital component for family stability. Third, the children of these parents grow up in economically stable environments, and they learn middle-class values such as marriage, education, and the capacity to earn money. In the psyche of the children, this value is real and accepted because they see their parents practicing these values, which makes it realistic and attainable. In most cases they know their parents have completed college or a professional degree and go off to work every day. Being exposed to the lesson that a good work ethic can increase chances for success, as well as not having any political or social barriers such as racism to deal with, the next generation of white people with good self-esteem can expect to have success. They will expect to complete college, perhaps attain a professional degree, land a well-paying job, get married, and set the stage for the success of the next generation of middle-class white people. In many cases the next generation of white people surpasses the middle class level and progresses even further in socioeconomic stature.

For a large percentage of black people, the journey is more difficult. Only a low percentage of black parents are married; a large number of children are raised in single, female-headed households. A large percentage of those single mothers are unemployed and rely on public assistance. The black man growing up with out a father or appropriate role model does not see the value of completing high school because although education was stressed to him by his parents, they are uneducated and not practicing this value themselves. His father abandoned the family when he was young, and because of this example he feels it is appropriate to abandon his children and their mother. He has little interest in joining the work force because he suffers from the reactionary psychosocial trauma that his father, grandfather, and great grandfather suffered through in terms of racism and discrimination. Subsequently, he sees the inner city drug trade as a viable option to generating an income. Because of this apathy, he doesn't even try to achieve anything constructive with his life. Finally he adopts a negative, self-destructive value system that only has status within the criminal realms of the black community, and this is what his children see and grow up to emulate, continuing the multigenerational perpetuation of the poor black lower class.

Nathan Brandon asserts,

> Taking responsibility for my happiness is empowering. It places my life back in my hands.
>
> I am responsible for accepting or choosing the values by which I live. If I live by values I have accepted or adopted passively and unthinkingly, it is easy to imagine that they are "just my nature", just who I am," and to avoid recognizing that choice is involved. If I am willing to recognize that choices and decisions are crucial when values are adopted, then I can take a fresh look at my values, question them, and if necessary revise them. Again, it is taking responsibility that sets me free.
>
> I am responsible for raising my self-esteem. Self-esteem is not a gift I can receive from someone else. It is generated from within. To wait passively for something to happen that will raise my self-esteem is to sentence myself to a life of frustration.

After illustrating all of the social, political, and economic reasons why black people suffer from collective low self-esteem as a community, Brandon points out great tool in which we can use to improve our self-esteem. It is presently the twenty-first century. The founding fathers of America understood that in order to successfully sever themselves from England and become autonomous, they needed to create a system that would outlast their own lives. They saw the need to have a system that was flexible and would accommodate the impending political, social, and economic changes that would inevitably occur through out the world. They knew that nothing stayed the same forever. Therefore when they drifted the American Constitution, they labeled it as a living document.

As indicated earlier, America has undergone a series of tremendous changes, particularly with the social policy of the American black population. Despite all of the mental and emotional scars we have accrued since the first slave ships arrived in Jamestown, Virginia, in the late fifteenth century, in this present day and for the first time in our history in America, we can take personal responsibility and pursue internal happiness for ourselves without any sociological barriers of past generations. We can mentally rid ourselves of the destructive value system we have adopted from the hood and conceptualize new and more productive values, passing them down to the next generation. When we take responsibility for our self-esteem, we no longer have to blame the white man for our misery because we now control the direction of our lives.

We do not have to accept a value system that is unthinking, passive, or even self-destructive, believing it is just our nature.

We can turn our lives around by mentally acknowledging that drug selling is no longer for us. Changing how we think ultimately leads to changing our behavior and conceiving a better outlook for our lives that does not include personal limitations; it is just as easily in our nature to be a successful college student, doctor, or attorney—something that maximizes our innate abilities. We can put our lives back in our hands. We can move away from negative friends and meet new, positive ones, being concerned with what someone thinks of us. We can be better parents to our children. We can get off public assistance and pursue a career using our abilities. Our emotional well-being can be independent of the validation of a man or woman in our lives. We can be responsible for promoting healthy self-esteem. Despite what we look, like despite our social economic backgrounds, strong self-esteem is a gift we can give to ourselves.

In this instance I feel it is not appropriate to be a passive observer in life, but to be proactive about decisions and actions. Instead of just allowing events to occur and play out and hope for the best, I can be the primary lead acting decision maker to help facilitate the outcome I desire. When I was in grade school and middle school, I saw the effects of this approach to life. Every time I was passive about something and let it play out, it did not usually work to my advantage. But on the few occasions when I consciously made the decision to be proactive about something and followed up with the decisive behavior, more often than not I experienced the outcome I wanted. That was long before I understood this philosophy on an intellectual level. When I was young, I had instances where I practiced it. If I had and exam and studied before it, I performed well. If I did not study, I usually failed. The concept of being proactive has served me well. I did not always have the result I wanted. However, most of the time I received the desired results. In addition, even when I did not succeed in something while being proactive, I still had the satisfaction of knowing I made a genuine and active effort to achieve that goal. My self-esteem greatly benefited from this idea. It is better to fail at something than to not attempt or to not try hard.

The post-civil rights generation is a great time to live in America. There are so many great opportunities available to black Americans, and it is up to us to shake off the mental slavery and the psychological alliance to destructive value systems. By being aware of who we are as self-valued individuals, we can be responsible for the everyday decisions of our lives. We can choose not to join gangs but to get vocational training and land a job in a field we love, receiving happiness from our labor.

Brandon states that "through work we support our existence. Through the exercise of our intelligence towards some use full ends, we become more fully human. Without productive goals and productive effort, we remain forever children." He goes on to say, "In any given context the mark of independence and self responsibility is the orientation that ask, what actions are possible to me? what needs to be done? How can I improve my condition? How can I move beyond this impasse? What will be the best use of my energies in this situation? Self-responsibility is expressed through an active orientation to life. It is expressed through the understanding that no one is here on earth to spare us the necessity of independence, and through the understanding that without work, independence is impossible."

The Need for Work

In order to discover what we are capable of doing and to create a purpose for our lives, we must embrace the need for work. I remember back in college attending one of the many pregraduation ceremonial dinners the Black Student Union offered to its graduating class. Dr. Leonard Jeffries was the keynote speaker, and years later I began to understand how profound and prophetic his statement was. He said, "When you graduate, don't get a job, get a mission." I now understand that when you are able to take a job about which you are passionate, it ceases to feel like work and is more of a pleasure to perform.

There are segments that exist in our community that do not value the idea of work. Even if it is never stated verbally, the passive way in which some people go about not working is indicative to how they feel. I remember being at work one day and hearing the comments of a black woman who was on public assistance and about to receive a WEP assignment: "I never worked in my life. My mother never worked nor did my grand mother. So how do they expect me to do a WEP assignment?" Unfortunately, this attitude is prevalent in our community.

I believe in the idea of work and all of the values it entail. Work is an expression that you exist, that you are alive and want to be recognized. Like a great artist or composer, your work is your testimony that you were here on this earth. People have and always will respect good work, and this becomes the card you present to people about the quality of your character. Work defines you, and you define it solely based on the arbitrary duties that you do.

Quality work nurtures your self-esteem because you have the satisfaction of knowing how great your capabilities are and the possibilities they can create for you. In order to manifest our identities and subsequently our destinies, we must be productive with our lives. This could be exemplified in any aspect of our lives; whether in school, on a job, in the community, or as a parent, we must show productivity for our efforts.

I fully understand that work does not come without its challenges, especially when you're doing something you do not like. But nonetheless, when you are in the work game, you are exposed to many rewarding options that can be taken advantage of. If you want to change careers, you can research which direction to go, and with a basic work ethic, you can increase the chances of success in the new field. This is much like being a college student. Very rarely do students enter four-year universities and graduate with the same ideas they had as a freshman. In an educational environment, one is exposed to so many new ideas that in many cases, one's fundamental philosophy of life can end up completely different.

With regard to the idea of work, college helped me in many ways. As mentioned earlier, my parents did not work, and I grew up on public assistance; I did not attain the value of a good work ethic from my parents, and in a lot of respects I was bright but lazy. When I got to college, in the early years I struggled a great deal because I had no time management skills and did not know how to focus on the work at hand. I thought that my good looks and charismatic personality would always make someone cut me some slack. After being disappointed in this area on a number of occasions, I finally learned that to assert my right to be respected as an individual and an adult; I had to complete quality work. One doesn't have to do great work 100 percent of the time, but it at least has to be an effort of quality. With this understanding I learned tools like time management and the ability to focus on the work at hand to get the job done. Professors finally respected me because I got their work done on time and did not give them any of the excuses I had used many times in the past.

While in college, I also met great thinkers who exposed me to new ideas and recommended various reading materials. Subsequently, when I graduated, the person I was prior to college no longer existed, and a new individual with a better understanding of who I was in this society emerged.

When I officially joined the work force, some of my old behaviors presented themselves in my work quality, but I think I understand why this was. I was working at Catholic Charities as a case manger for the mentally ill and chemical abusing population. I did not want that job, but it was the only job that hired me, and I had life responsibilities to address. I was not happy, but what really hurt me was my inability to focus on what I needed to do at that moment. I was too busy thinking, "When I leave this job, this will happen. When I leave this job I will do that." My future plans had nothing to do with the quality of my work I should have performed while employed with Catholic Charities. As I moved on to other jobs, I slowly began to learn this lesson, and it assisted me throughout my professional life. I began to improve the quality of my work and practice it on a consistent basis.

Another issue that lead to a valuable life lesson arose. During my younger years, in preparation for college, I always assumed I would became a lawyer. In the eighties I watched shows like *LA Law*, and Hollywood always made being a lawyer look exiting, fun, and of course lucrative. My very first major at St. Augustine's College was criminal justice. I did not take any specific law classes during that academic year, but I took some mandatory sociology courses needed for my major. I fell in love with sociology and all of its related components. The textbooks were incredibly interesting readings, and it seemed I was a natural for the materials. The concepts came so easily to me that studying for exams was pleasurable. Subsequently, I did very well in all of my sociology work at the undergraduate and graduate level.

I began to take specific law classes during my sophomore and junior years, and I did okay. I studied hard for the work, but the material did not come as easily as the sociology work, and it was not as interesting. I found law boring and needed a lot of effort just to get to one solution. But I pressed on thinking that someday I was going to be a lawyer. My mother's influence played a significant role; she always wanted me to be a lawyer and stated that she thought I would make a good one.

After college I moved to New York City and took the LSAT in the fall of 1996—and did terribly. This was a tremendous blow to my intellectual confidence. That in itself was an ominous sign, but I reasoned that all I had to do was work harder, and I would get in to law school somewhere. I never took the LSAT again; instead I applied and got accepted to graduate school at Long Island University as a political science major. I reasoned that the curriculum had a great balance of sociology, administrative, and law courses to give me the edge for another law school attempt. But just like in undergrad, my natural instinctual pattern revealed itself again. I did extremely well in all of the sociology courses and did just adequately in the law courses. I realized at this point that law school was not in the cards, but I figured that I could still be in the law field in some kind of way. In the spring of 2003 I signed up for a program at Monroe College to attain a certificate to become a certified paralegal. The course was for twelve weeks, and I barely lasted three. The reading material was so boring and ridged that I lost interest and never returned to the course.

Finally the last straw was my stint working with the Brooklyn Treatment Court in the winter of 2005. Again I reasoned that although I was not a lawyer, I could be related to the field in some sort of way. The job entailed criminal case management done much like a parole officer, and it included a great deal of interaction with attorneys and judges. Within a month I knew I did not fit in. The work was so inflexible and ridged, and with the way my brain works, I need to be flexible and creative with my thinking. I worked very hard to be successful at that job, but I totally bombed, and mercifully they fired me after six months of service.

During the time I was unemployed and job hunting, I read numerous self-esteem books such as Minchinton's

Maximum Self Esteem as well as *The Fountainhead* by Ayn Rand. The self-help books promoted being my natural true self and following my own self-defined interests despite all opposition; you're my work would speak for me. After increasing my self-esteem to (for me) unprecedented levels, I finally knew I had the inner strength to say I do not want to be a lawyer. I had the confidence to assert that sociology was my thing, and I wanted to spend my life teaching and helping people become the best they could be.

Both the good and bad experiences have been great for me because it taught me how to address adversity. Without those experiences, I would never have fully embraced my true interest and allowed the passion for what I do direct the quality of my work.

The concept of work was always a challenge for my mother. As I mentioned earlier, when I was very young she did work for a time with the post office. However later on in life, she told me that due to a her poor performance and excessive absenteeism, she was fired from her position. With her self-esteem really low and a weak concept of personal responsibility, she did not seek more work and instead applied for and stayed on welfare for many years. Her attitude at the time was blaming other people for her problems. She did not know how to take responsibility for the fact that she got herself fired, and by not immediately returning to the workforce, she further damaged her personal and professional development. She missed out on at least three life lessons that could have altered the course of her life and her thinking. The first is her professional growth and development. When my mother worked at the post office, it was the late sixties and early seventies. At least twelve or thirteen years went by before my mother took on her next job as a receptionist with Boston City Hospital. She worked there while I was in grades eight and nine. I remember her always coming home and complaining about how someone in authority would criticize her performance and give her a hard time. She ended up leaving that job because she could not take the demanding pressure of the position any longer, and she went back to public assistance. I assert that if she had that gone back into the work force as soon as she had lost the post office position—and not wasted more than a decade being idle—she would undoubtedly has learned the tools necessary to manage a difficult work environment. By not working all that time, she fell out of practice and lost all work environment etiquette.

Perhaps the biggest miscue my mother made was the detrimental message she sent to her children. As a result, when he was younger, my oldest brother Glen always had a problem holding down jobs. From part-time, after-school jobs to quitting high school and working full time, he a terrible time being punctual and productive. He was fired from positions several times, and interestingly enough, my mother would criticize him for losing jobs in the same manner that she lost hers.

Glen finally attained a very good work ethic after he got older and realized that the only way to attain money and keep a job was to be productive. He learned this lesson after some earlier scrapes with the law and a relatively short stint of substance abuse. Unfortunately, as he got sicker and was nearing the end of life, he was no longer capable of staying healthy for long periods of time and had to take multiple sick days off. The mind was willing and super human effort was there, but his body could no longer function at the high level to which he was accustomed.

I mentioned earlier how I struggled with the concept of a good work ethic and subsequently had to learn it outside my mother's home. My youngest brother Parrish was a little different from the rest of us. He saw the handwriting on the wall as young as seventeen or eighteen, always keeping a summer job. He had the best work ethic out of all of us at the time, and I picked up a great deal of work etiquette lessons from him.

The second lesson my mother missed out on was interacting with positive, upwardly mobile black people. I mentioned earlier that my mother, like so many other blacks, suffers from a psychological condition of self-hatred because we live in a white supremacist world and everything about us viewed through that lens is negative. My mother's own rough childhood, her disappointing relationships with men, and her own willful decision to socialize with black people that also hustled and did not work for a living—these events led her to develope an intense enmity for black people. The hypocritical irony was that she practiced many of the behaviors she criticized, When I brought this to her attention, she would yell at me—a manifestation of her weak self-esteem and no concept of personal responsibility. She did not have the ability to see herself as the primary active player in the poor decisions she made.

By taking herself out of the work force, she only saw the worst of what black people have to offer, and she herself was very much a part of that world of hustlers. My mother actively engaged in all the negative values that are such an integral part of the underworld of the black community, such as cheating, deceit, stealing, and back-stabbing,. However she would blame black people when she became the victim of these values, instead of seeing her role that helped create the situation. She did not stay in the work force long enough to meet the numerous educated and morally ethical blacks. This group of blacks was in an entirely different world from hers, and subsequently she did not learn many new lessons in life.

I realized a long time ago that the primary difference between the viewpoints of my mother's and mine is the fact that I went to college. In particular I did my freshman and sophomore years of college at a historically black school in the south—a Plessy versus Ferguson institution, as I refer to them. At the school 90 percent of the faculty were black professors with their PhDs. There I saw young black students like myself working toward a college education. Interestingly enough, many of them were second generation college students.

When I entered in the work force, again I saw educated blacks such as myself who did not subscribe to the negative values of some of the members in our community. I'm not saying they were perfect people to work with, but I did not have the bad experiences with black people about which my mother so often complained. In fact to this day most of my negative experiences still come from white people.

In addition, because of my many positive black male role models and my intense research to learn about black people (and subsequently myself), I developed a strong sense of black pride that was absent during my childhood. Because my mother did not have my experiences and educational training, she does not share the same perspective on black people.

Although I do look at the world through "black-colored glasses," I am not naïve to the inappropriate behavior of so-called educated blacks. Even in the work environment, some of us still have to challenge the boundaries of what's acceptable behavior. Nonetheless, because of my education and training, I was always able to identify and isolate the behavior as an individual act and not a broad strike against my entire race.

The third lesson my mother could have learned is on a personal note. Because she did not immediately go back to work, she missed out on potentially meeting a more suitable life partner. Because she was an active player in the hustle world, the only types of men she met were hustlers. Even though she wanted this to happen, it is absolutely unfathomable to think a single black mother of three in the ghetto could land an honest man with the integrity to take care of her and her family by drawing from this horrible selection. Every man my mother dealt with was the same as my father: an uneducated hustler with low self-esteem and no concept of personal responsibility. Theoretically, if she had remained in the work force on a consistent basis, the likelihood of meeting a more honorable man would have increased.

Because my mother made those fateful decisions, her thinking never fully evolved, and she stayed mentally stagnant with ineffective life philosophies. As I said earlier, my mother on the surface is a very intelligent woman. However it was her poor self-esteem that led to poor decisions, which in turn never allowed her to fully develop or actualize her fullest potential.

Needing Societal Approval as Black People

As black people we stand out significantly from other people in American society. As illustrated earlier, we are highly identifiable in our appearance due to what would be considered radically different features by the white standard of approval. Due to the history of how we have been treated and our socialization, it is construed that we behave, act, or even think differently from the majority culture. However is that really a negative thing, and should we be ashamed of our appearance, most of which we cannot control? Also, as long as long as it is not illegal or criminally deviant, is the type of music, choice in clothes, or style of hair something we should suffer for?

Another taboo topic is the idea of colorism in the black community. It has been over 140 years since the Emancipation Proclamation, and we have been psychologically damaged to the point that today we still believe that being light skinned is recognized as being more attractive and thus more acceptable to the majority society. White people are more comfortable around light-skinned blacks than darker skinned ones. Even in contemporary times, we still hold onto false standards of beauty, and having children with white people allows us to have the arbitrary definition of "pretty babies."

Latin American blacks have been adversely affected by this psychological phenomenon. For the past hundred years, Latin American blacks have had an open practice of miscegenation with their former white slave masters. My theory is as follows: Latin American blacks are and have been very poor in their respective countries of origin during and after slavery. In these countries there existed a similar social code that acknowledged the white race as being the more superior and powerful race. However, there were several different social practices regarding race interaction. In the United States, there was always a clear and defined social line that separated the races and that was enforced by law, racism, social taboo codes, and in extreme cases, violence; this is illustrated in Jim Crow and the Black Codes.

After Latin American blacks were freed from slavery in the late nineteenth century, there weren't any specific legal codes that kept the races apart—but there were social customs. With perpetually weak economic conditions that also affected the newly arrived Spanish and Portuguese immigrants, this allowed poor whites to live alongside poor blacks in the same communities. For Latin American blacks, being poor, black, and a member of the lesser powered race—and not having any significant race pride movements—made them subconsciously believe that a great deal of their economic and social problems lied in the fact that they were black. They knew that that it was impossible to change their physical appearance, and therefore they willingly engaged in a practice of miscegenation with the majority white population, under the false notion that the different races were equal. The goal was and still is to produce children that would be recognized as white, beautiful, and socially acceptable to the majority culture. The hope was that because the children were lighter, perhaps they would be exposed to more educational and social opportunities than their parents. They also rationalized that the children would face significantly less discrimination from the dominant white Spanish and Portuguese cultures. In addition, Latin America also has a long and deep history of prostitution that undoubtedly played a significant role in the skin color of present-day blacks in this region. With this genetically altered appearance, they could achieve a level of acceptance and approval from the dominant white society.

I do understand that in reality we have our choices and preferences, and there is nothing wrong with that. In fact the premise of self-esteem is to have the inner strength to be able to make the desired choices that we want for ourselves. I'm only pointing out that oftentimes our choices are influenced by societal standards; it is on such deep subconscious level that it feels natural to believe we made our choices independently. However the reality is our social milieu and circumstances have more often than not dictated what we prefer and do not prefer.

I teach this same lesson in my class, in which I challenge my students to understand why they make the choices they make. This is a concept that I drill in their heads, and I hope that one day, as with my academic and life lessons, it will click.

When I discuss needing societal approval, I am only referring to racial appearance and cultural behavior. As stated earlier, we do live in unprecedented times in which we can attend the best schools, attain work at the best places of employment, and live where we want to live. On a social, practical level we as a community need educational approval. We need to complete high school with the best grades possible to get into the best universities possible and have an economic impact on society with our increasingly strong presence in the work force. Not needing societal approval does not make us exempt from social responsibilities of this nature. Nonetheless, being socially responsible and needing to fit into the acceptance model of white America's social standard are two entirely different things. One of the main disadvantages of a conscious attempt to be something we naturally are not is that it is not going to work. Racism is still alive and well despite all of our progress. Most white people do not have a high opinion of blacks to begin with. Remember that most white people are middle class even though they are shinking percentage wise and moving towards the working poor. They have had little or no interaction with black people especially in white homogeneous suburban communities. Stereotypes and negative media images are their main vessels used to formulate an opinion. With very few exceptions most whites will at the least have some kind of unconscious racism, in which they will at times say something racially inappropriate, behave condescendingly, or make an outright racist comment and later apologize for the offense.

The October 17, 2007 edition of the New York Daily news contained a small article printed in the world news section. The name of the article was "Long Island Scientist in Race Flap."

> London—A Nobel Prize—winning geneticist based on long island is embroiled in controversy after telling a British newspaper that Black people are less intelligent than white people. James Watson, 79, told the Sunday Times that he was inherently gloomy about the prospect of Africa because all our, social policies are based on

the fact that their intelligence is the same as ours where as all the testing says not really . . . He said there is a natural desire to consider all human beings equal, but people who have to deal with black employees find this not true.

This is the opinion of a prominent scientist in the twenty-first century, not the eighteenth or nineteenth century. The ideology that people of African decent are inherently less intelligent, although no longer as overt, is still widely believed. James Watson is not some poorly educated redneck cracker from the back woods of Alabama or Georgia who is threatened by the social progress of black people. He is a Nobel Peace Prize—winning genetic scientist with a wide audience to influence. The reality is far to many white people still think the same as he does and completely agree with his assertion, even if it is politically incorrect or unpopular to verbalize nowadays.

When you try to act outside of yourself and be something whites want you to be, you perform a great disservice to yourself. It is the same as the old minstrel images of the slavery and Jim Crow eras. During these times, because black people were all but powerless to the circumstances surrounding them, they had to perform entertainment for white people for their livelihoods and their safety, to make whites less uncomfortable around blacks. However even with the singing, dancing, placating, and submission, whites still looked at blacks as subhuman and beastly. More than one hundred years later, some whites still carry the notion that they are the superior race, and they still maintain such a derogatory idea about descendents of the African race.

What I am suggesting is this: Like what you like. Enjoy what you like to enjoy. Receive pleasure from what you want to receive pleasure. If your personal taste runs along the lines of heavy metal to country western, this is fine as long as you genuinely receive pleasure from this these types of music. But do not be afraid to enjoy artistic expression indigenous to the black community as well. Many Blacks feel that in certain environments they can gain white approval by repudiating artistic and cultural forms of black expression. It does not matter what someone does to assuage or accommodate the thinking of certain whites—in the minds of the social white supremacist, we are still inferior. Instead, be proud of your appearance. Be proud that you enjoy an art form that is different from the mainstream society. Be proud that your speech is just as intelligent, even if it is different from most white people's. We are free to choose who we like in our lives. This is the beauty of life, that we have choices. Nonetheless, choose a potential partner based on the fact that he or she treats you with love and respect, not on skin color, straight hair, and the potential of having a light-skinned baby. In essence, be proud to be black.

The advantage to not wanting or needing the approval of white people and their standard of what's appropriate is that we are comfortable being ourselves. We are not manipulated by them and we set our own rules, ideas, and standards of how we live our lives. Some whites are not going to accept us anyway, but that is not important. What is important is that we accept ourselves and live our lives as we see fit.

While growing up, I had a best friend named Chris Madden. Chris was really light skinned and looked as if he was a mulatto, but the beautiful part is that his acknowledgement of our friendship was as genuine as mine was. He never insulted me or made me feel uncomfortable, even though it was clear that economically his family was significantly better off than mine. I always felt welcomed in his home, and his mother treated me as if I were one of her sons. Chris's biological father did not play a big role in his life; in fact I do not know if Chris even saw him on a regular basis. Nonetheless, he was reared in an extended family structure. His grandparents, who owned the house they lived in; his mother; three brothers and a sister; his aunt and her daughter; and his disabled uncle. All of the adults worked, and therefore there were multiple resources in their house for them to draw upon. Everyone in his family would treat me as if I was one of their own. This analysis in not about him but about me and my weak level of self-esteem at the time.

Chris was better at certain things than I was. He was a better athlete, a better basketball player, and a better student than I was, and because his skin was so light, he was considered better looking.

During some of my family's most difficult economic times, I would become really depressed, and I did not understand it at the time. I was in the seventh grade and lived across town in another part of the city called Hyde Park. Chris and most of the friends I hung out with lived in the Dorchester area of Boston. Every Saturday I would take a thirty-minute bus ride to Chris's house and hang with him. We would play basketball or stay at his house and watch TV. His family would always give me a meal. The reality was my family was struggling so badly that I knew that that was the most nourishing and satisfying meal I would receive during my week.

At least once a month, I would call from his house and ask my mother if I could spend the night. She would be resistant to the idea but would eventually give in. I knew what I was doing: I would wait till it became late for a thirteen-year-old boy to ride public transportation by himself, and then I would call home and ask. I knew I would get a great dinner and a great breakfast Sunday morning. After a while, my mother would ask me why I always wanted to stay at Chris's house. I think even though she would not admit it, perhaps I was embarrassing her as a parent. At that point I certainly was not aware of it. Nonetheless, the reality was I hated my own house and wanted to be at Chris's, and my reasoning was this: Chris appeared to be everything I wanted to be. He was light skinned and good looking. He had a great, functional, middle-class family that lived with middle-class values. Chris always had money and seemed to never be in need of something. Conversely I was dark skinned and not regarded as good looking. I was ashamed of my family because my mother did not work. We were on welfare and were constantly in need of money. My family was not functional. My father did not work and only came by periodically. I was always broke, and other kids began to recognize and tease me about it. Due to my mother's open promiscuity, I never had a strong sense of family pride or self-value. Being with and around Chris provided me with a vicarious lifestyle into which I escaped every Saturday, and I always tried to prolong the experience as much as possible.

Those were some difficult times emotionally and psychologically; it's still hard for me to address it even now, almost thirty years later. Being poor and part of a dysfunctional family is not fun, and I must admit I'm still traumatized by the experience. My self-esteem as a young man was in shambles because everything in my reality provided sufficient evidence that I did not matter. Chris's presence in my life was proof that not all black people suffered socially and economically as my family did. I did not realize it, but his family model gave me hope on a subconscious level that I was not cursed to live like this.

Dealing with Personal Emotional Pain

As an adult it appeared that despite my obvious academic success, great work ethic, and willingness to always joke around because of my personality type, on a personal level I always carried around a heavy bag of emotional pain from my past and the trauma of growing up the way that I did. I was not alone. My youngest brother Parrish carried with him the same painfully emotional baggage for several years.

It was the type of pain that you believe is a part of your DNA, that arbitrarily arrests any free feelings of happiness that you may experience at any given time. Because I allowed it to persist and had no frame of reference or knowledge that I could change it, I believed that I was sentenced to a lifetime of periodical depression. A sadness would arrive unannounced like an unwanted guest. I knew it was not good for my emotional well-being but took it in because I felt it was my duty. Fortunately I have since learned otherwise.

This concept is not lost on the collective psyche of black people. Other so-called successful blacks I have met assert the same thing about periodic depression and sadness. The interesting phenomenon is that especially in college, many of the friends I attained over the years did not experience the hardcore way of living that I did while growing up. On several occasions, they had both parents present in their lives and never really saw a hardship in their lives. I am certain that their family lives were not perfect, however they did not have to worry about when their next meal was arriving. Nonetheless, that pervasive feeling of periodical and sometimes chronic depression would creep into their thinking.

The core beliefs of having healthy self-esteem is challenging and then dismissing all the ineffective and mythical life-coping lessons we have been socialized with, and having the courage to open our minds to new ideas about self-improvement and feeling good about ourselves. If you look back at black history and the way we were socialized about how to respond to certain stimuli, we can somewhat understand how living with emotional pain still affects us more than a century later. Upon being captured from Africa and being stripped of every indigenously African emotional coping mechanism, we became psychologically naked. Our entire mental frame of reference was that of an African person, because up until that point that's what we were psychologically, spiritually, and socially. It was forbidden for us to practice our natural belief system and worship our cultural god or gods, as was taught to us for millennia before the slave trade. That human emotional void was purposely filled by the white man's inculcation of Christianity to the black slaves.

Just like all of our forced social inferiority complexes, Christianity informed us that we all are born into a world of sin and have fallen short of the glory of God. It implied that to reach this glory, we had to endure great levels of emotional pain and suffering in order to be cleansed in the name of God. Because of the depiction of Jesus Christ being crucified and reborn, this became a psychological symbol and justification for black suffering.

As an example, I remember once as a kid that there was no food to eat in the house. We were hungry, and I suspected that I was frustrated that we had to suffer events such as this from time to time. My mother, feeling powerless, offered a sort of biblical explanation as to why this happened to us every now and then. She said, "God makes the decision on if we eat or not." This translated to me as so sort of holy anointment test of faith that we had to suffer through in order to be recognized by God. At the time I bought that, and my mother fully convinced me that this was God's will that we had no food. It was certainly not the fact that she did not work or that the welfare check was late in this particular instance.

Because Christianity was not our native religion or belief system, and someone else forced it on us, we accepted it because the reality of the master-slave relationship revealed and confirmed who was in power. Slaves had no power over their lives or the lives of their families, and the white slave master wielded limitless power over them, including the decision on which slaves suffered and which ones did not. The slave master was almost an extension of God because he even had control over the life or death of a slave. The white man taught slaves through the Bible that it was their natural state to suffer and be ruled by the white race. He taught them that they should not seek to rebel or revolt because even though they were suffering in pain now, when they died, God would reward them in heaven for their loyalty to him and the white race.

I argue that this religious sociological/historical part of our history plays a role as to why black people continue to suffer from emotional pain today. In most cases it is a conscience decision to do so. Why do we experience unwarranted levels of guilt in our collective psyche? It's almost as if some type of internal alarm was programmed into us and would go off anytime we would began to enjoy our lives and feel happy without feeling guilty. It was as if we always had to view our lives through endless struggle, and to struggle was good and humble in the eyes of God. If you were happy and guilt free, it meant you were backsliding and implied that you were doing something immoral and needed to repent.

This is a fact: black people were not Christians until the slave trade. Christianity was forced upon us and used as an additional psychological weapon of submission to keep us subdued and to accept our place as servants to white race. It was a form of mental castration. Over the years I have brought up this undeniable piece of history to explain some of our behaviors to academics and clergy, and to this day I have not received a satisfactory retort. This is because the hegemony of white supremacy prevents them from understanding this delicate point because of its opposite affect on them. Quite simply, Christianity and white supremacy allowed them to have and develop a functional sense of self-esteem.

I do acknowledge that Christianity has played a significant role in holding together the moral structure of the black community over the generations. In addition I also am not advocating black people stop worshiping a religion we have been worshiping for more than a quarter of a millennium. The beauty of life is that we have the freedom to choose whatever it is we want to spiritually nurture us.

What I am advocating is for black people to no longer be afraid to think outside the box and ask certain questions our naturally inquisitive minds want to ask but are injected with fear to impede such challenging queries. I am unequivocally against fear-based religious or spiritual teachings that keep one mentally locked in a cage and unable to grow intellectually.

Nonetheless, I will state this: On a personal level I am not a Christian. In fact, I do not think Christianity works for black people or descendants of the African race on a large scale. Christianity is supposed to be a unifier, however in reality it seems that Christianity actually makes black people hate other black people from different ethnic backgrounds. The only unification it achieves within the divided ethnic camps is that it makes us love and seek to unify with white people and white supremacy. On multiple occasions I have heard ethnic blacks make derogatory comments about another black group. American blacks and West Indian blacks in New York City have well-known and publicized conflicts and divides. Even blacks from Africa that immigrated to the United States have displayed disdain against American blacks. In addition, lighter skinned Latinos continue to practice open acts of discrimination against darker skinned Latinos and West Indian blacks.

What do all these groups have in common? Most of them are subscribers to the Christian faith and have a stronger desire to get along with the dominant white race and culture. Granted these are for economic, social, and political advantage reasons; however even members of these groups from the lower economic rungs believe in the implied and imagined deficiencies of the others and subsequently maintain a deep social distance.

I assert that a belief system should work for you in this world, and the offense I charge Christianity with is that, with a few exceptions of success, black Christians across the globe are the poorest of the poor and the least empowered. From Louisiana to Haiti to Johannesburg to Rio Dejanaro, black Christians live and continue to live in the most deplorable conditions. To me this is a clear reality that the religion does not work on a large scale for members of the African race.

Personally, Christianity has not worked for me as a philosophy of enhancing my self-esteem—in fact it did the opposite, reinforcing how bad I was, that I was born in sin, and that there was nothing I could do outside of accepting the presence of an entity I could not see or touch to change my life. In addition, I was not a productive person under the doctrine of Christianity because I was too reliant on something other than myself to make my life better.

When I was younger I was a practicing Christian and became born again. However, nothing happened that profoundly changed my life. I was still suffering from low self-esteem and depression, I still had bad parents, and I still lived in a dangerous crime-ridden neighborhood. My reality changed when I learned that I had to rely on my brain and my efforts for my personal well-being. I have since not looked back.

Christianity fosters psychological guilt that was not present in our race prior to the slave trade. Christianity taught us that the pursuit of pleasure and happiness was a sin and therefore wrong in the eyes of God. We were doomed to a life time of emotional suffering until the day we died. Meanwhile the descendants of the white race still had significant levels of emotional stability because they knew society and God was a reflection of them and how they looked.

The concept of Christianity and God is supposed to be against killing. However former President George Bush prayed to God in the hope of killing perceived enemies of the United States. American whites accept this and view this as Christian and American. These are unarguable examples of how Christianity works for one group and not the entire globe.

Over time I learned, through the philosophy of self-esteem enhancement, that I was not born in sin; I had a right to be happy about my life and existence. I rejected Christianity's "anti me" doctrine and continued to learn the tools of living with integrity and consequential thinking and decision making. I am the e master of the quality of my life, and I began to have far more success thinking and living like this because I accepted the basic concept that my life is my responsibility and no one else's, and my success and happiness was based on how far my brain took me. My brain created the ideas, scenarios, options, and actions of solutions to address whatever dilemma or issue I faced in my life. Christianity made me rely on something other than my brain; the philosophy of self-esteem made me love and trust my brain because in reality it created all of my success.

Minchinton states,

> We accept emotional pain with a certain amount of fatalism. We hear people express their belief that these negative emotions are natural and that everybody feels them. Since others' behaviors appears to bear this out, we accept it as true. Emotional pain *is* normal-in the sense that many or most people experience it. However, since experiencing disturbing emotions is a matter of choice, we can hardly consider it inevitable. To say a course of action is inevitable implies there are no alternatives, and there are optional ways of responding other than painfully.

> Pain is not intended to be anyone' way of life; it is nature's warning device to let us know something is wrong. Its only purpose is to direct our attention to any of our being that needs to be changed. To respond appropriately to pain, we look for its cause and finding it, eliminate it along with the negative energy it generated. We accept this warning when the pain is physical in nature, so we look for cures or treatments, and we seek relief till we find it.

> Because we have been conditioned to think emotional pain is unavoidable, rather than trying to remove its cause, we approach it with the idea of learning to tolerate it. However just as physical pain is indicates a physical condition that needs correction, emotional

pain points to errors in thinking and urges us to correct them. Obviously, then we can eliminate emotional pain by changing our thoughts about whatever is troubling us.

The Dangers of Emotional Pain

We all have to deal with emotional pain at some point in our lives. What's important is how we handle emotional pain and what tools we use to minimize, reduce, or even eliminate it from our lives. There are constructive ways to productively eliminate emotional pain and suffering in the form of depression, sadness, and general feelings of worthlessness.

Especially in the black community, all too often we judge our existence based on the value that others place on us. As mentioned earlier, black men are more susceptible to peer pressure and a desire to fit in. Based on what might be going on in the home, the present level of self-esteem, and the existing coping mechanisms determines how they handle emotional distress.

There are different forms of emotional stress, however the most dangerous for black men are fear, anger, and melancholy.

One of the definations of fear is, "A feeling of alarm or disquiet caused by awareness or expectation of danger." Growing up in the urban ghettos of America as a young black man equips one with a heightened sense of fear as an alarm and stimulates the very basic instinct for self-preservation.

Fear can be based on living under very onditions, from homicidal drug dealers to desperate drug addicts to racist police. It is not limited to fear of violent and abusive parents, of physical confrontations with the neighborhood or school bully, or of nothing to eat or your family being evicted from your home. You can have a fear of learning in school by asking a simple question, all because a teacher embarrassed you once, and subsequently you no longer ask questions because you do not want to feel that way again.

Over time a consistent exposure to these experiences can have a mentally conditioning effect on how one views the world. Based on these experiences, the outside world is perceived as dangerous and something to be avoided as much as possible. The fear creates a decision-making response that fosters choices that limit negative and unwanted encounters. This may include avoiding certain streets or blocks in a neighborhood even though that street may be a main artery for travel. One might avoid all forms of interaction with the police, or not want to go home because of dangerous parents. One might fear being mocked or ridiculed at school or forced into street fights.

As noted in the definition, fear is a warning system that alerts you to imminent danger, and it should be recognized as such. Our fear does protect us, however as we grow up, how will we learn not to fear new experiences, people, and places? How will we learn not to be afraid to adopt a new philosophy or to try a new way of thinking? How will we learn to unconditionally love people and what they can offer to our lives?

This is how I deal with periodic moments of unwanted depression. Whenever I feel the negative disposition creeping into my consciousness, I actively fight it with rational thoughts. I ask myself, "Is this real, and is it necessary to feel this way? Is it justified—what have I done to allow myself to feel like this?" Then I combat it with reality and rational thought. I ask myself, "Is my health good? Yes. Am I employed? Yes. Did I do anything to subject myself to this feeling? No." I consciously wage an internal battle until my conscious brain wins and ends the depression. I do not take on unearned guilt and will not allow irrational, depressed thoughts affect my consciousness. After practice this mental exercise works well for me.

Because I personally have had success with this exercise, I will go against a hundred years of modern psychiatry and assert that the conscious mind is stronger than the subconscious mind. If you suffer from bad dreams, you must remember that they are the same as bad memories: they only have power if you abdicate your power to them. Your conscious mind will always follow what you want it to do, and to me that is far more powerful than worrying about interpreting a nightmare and what it may mean. In reality the nightmare is quite ineffective in the real world of conscious thought.

I grew up attending the public school system in the city of Boston, and as you can guess most of my teachers were white. Up until the third grade I was an A student and really did not have any negative experiences with my teachers. I lived in the black community, and as children the only white people we really saw were the ones on TV or the police. However, as a child I did not have any negative run-ins with the police. I did not see crowds of black people be arrested or become the victims of violent acts. In fact, as a kid, the police were oftentimes nice and would always say hi back to us. They never initiated the greeting, but they always responded in kind. My mother and other adults, on the other hand, did not have kind words to describe the police in our neighborhood.

As I started getting older and got past the third grade, my grades began to slip and I started to develop that distinctly urban black bad attitude. I guess as I was aging, on some level I began to process my surroundings and acted accordingly with the world around me. This was also when I first started to curse and use the word nigger as a pronoun or adjective. From that point on my school environment and inner city social interactions began to change. As I struggled through school. the white teachers were no longer supportive and became abusive. By the time I was in the seventh or eighth grade, the public school teachers were socially racist. They would make anti-black remarks as effortlessly as if they were putting on their shirts to come to work that morning. In addition, without any provocation the white police officers would stop and harass my friends and me while we were going to school, walking down the street, or waiting at the bus stop.

I remember one time while I was in high school. My friends and I were heavily into hip hop music and had just made a cassette tape of us rapping, mixing, and scratching on a Sunday afternoon. In those days boom boxes were in style, and we were walking in the street playing our newly created beats and rhymes. We were aware of the fact that it was downtown Boston and that it was Sunday; there fore when we arrived at the walking concourse of the Prudential Building, we turned the box off.

With the radio still off, we ended up walking into a record store called Strawberries to browse at the music on display. I should mention that it was seven of us young black males going into that store in all-white downtown Boston. Next thing we knew, out of nowhere about twenty police officers ran in to the store, physically roughed us up, and arrested us. We were taken to the police station downtown and officially charged with disorderly conduct. Some racist white person apparently saw a group of black youths, got scared, and called the police. I'll never forget the lie they tried to place on us. They said we were walking around terrorizing the people in the strip mall. After a few trips to court, the judge finally dropped the case against us. Meanwhile we had missed several days of school, and our parents that worked had to take time off from the job to address those bogus and racist charges.

Understand the psychosis and the conditioning that took place in my brain at that time: from ordinary white people not liking me because I'm black, to racist police that falsely arresting innocent black youngsters on a quiet Sunday afternoon. You know they would not have done that to a group of white youths, even if they were being disorderly. The racist judge ultimately had to dismiss the case simply because there was no evidence against us. However, he could have ended the case on the first day, and because he didn't, we had to miss several days of school to straighten that mess out. We never should have been stopped, harassed, and arrested to begin with.

Circumstances like this conditioned me to fear and hate white people. As I got older and went off to college, in particular at Fairly Dickerson University, because of my conditioning I expected that the white people there would be the same as I had encountered in Boston. Unfortunately, for the most part they were. However, there were some good, nonracist white people there as well. Professor Ron Jawarski was one of the first white people who treated me the same as any white student in his class. He respected my opinions and guided my thinking and intellectual development the way a good professor should. In fact, he planted the seed that blossomed into my love of sociology as a vehicle to understand how societies work.

If I did not open my mind to new experiences, and had continued to view all white people as the same, I never would have received the full installment of love for sociology and have trusted Professor Jawarski with my fragile academic development. He also provided great life advice from a perspective that proclaimed that all human beings were equal. I really enjoyed speaking with him during his office hours, because minus the racism that black people almost exclusively have to deal with, he had experienced many of the adolescent challenges I had faced. He would share some of his success and failures with me, and he inspired me to be the best I could be.

It is a societal reality that everyone experiences the emotions of anger and bitterness from time to time. Whether someone is disappointed by an event that was beyond his or her control, we are socialized by the American culture to respond in a way that merits some sort of emotional outburst. This in itself is a ubiquitous experience. However for black males, in particular young ones, this is particularly detrimental. This group's explosive emotional responses can lead to a lifetime of bad choices and consequences that include extreme circumstances such as jail, injuries for life, and death.

Jerry Minchinton explains the origins of emotional pain.

> From child hood on we have been surrounded by examples of other persons reacting similarly to their environment. Too many popular songs glorify emotional pain, telling us heartbreak and suffering are inevitable, and we should expect to put up with all kinds of abusive treatment and emotional pain, supposedly in the name of love. The soap operas and romantic fiction flooding the market encourage us to believe emotional anguish and agony are nothing exceptional, just par for the course.

> Considering the many incorrect and harmful beliefs about emotion we have absorbed, it is small wonder we are so often upset, angry or depressed. Like our other false beliefs, we have assimilated these so thoroughly they seem like unquestionable facts instead of the unsupported and inaccurate assumptions they actually are.

> No matter how we look at it, this is undeniably a peculiar belief. Although there is absolutely no reason why we should make ourselves feel unhappy when reality turns out to be different from what we wanted, this is exactly what we do. When matters don't go as we hope they will, rather than accept it with a smile,

we punish our selves with painful feelings. We respond to disappointments with tears, rage, or depression. We beat ourselves up because things aren't the way we want them to be.

We accept emotional pain with a certain amount of fatalism. We hear people express their belief that these negative emotions are natural and that everybody feels them. Since other's behavior appears to bear this out we accept it as true.

How people emotionally respond to an outside stimulus is a direct reflection of their self-esteem level at that time. It is a reflection on how they see themselves and how they view the world. Whether the world is friendly or hostile, inviting or exclusive, nurturing or emasculating, safe or dangerous, the decisions one can make based on the circumstance of the emotional state can make all the difference in the world in terms of the outcome of someone's life.

As mentioned earlier, this is especially difficult for black men. Due to weak levels of self-esteem, black men who succumb to overwhelming feelings of uncontrolled emotions face the risk of compounding the situation and making it worse with a negative reaction. Those negative reactions can lead to self-destructive and dangerous consequences. The behavior is an inner impression fueled by a morbid sense that one's life is not worth living.

Violent behavior with secret wishes to die is often exemplified in contemporary hip hop music and videos. Titles such as "Ready to Die" by the late Notorious BIG, the alias, "Makiaveli" used by the late Tupac Shakur, and "The

Massacre" by 50 Cent pay homage to the proverbial fallen street soldier or hustler and are reflective of a precarious inner city value system. Even in the art form of hip hop, which I love, I cannot support or endorse these themes or concepts of ways of living. To me they are antilife, and my life is the most important thing to me, as yours should be to you. Those are concepts that do not prepare you for embracing your life but ultimately throwing it away.

The newspapers and TV news are full of stories that illustrate the consequences of the most extreme examples of negative, uncontrolled, emotional responses. In addition, most African Americans have been (or know someone that has been) involved in a dangerous situation because of uncontrolled anger or other emotions.

Not too long ago, during the course of this writing, my friends and I experienced a tragedy. One of our friends who resided in another state appeared to have committed a murder-suicide. Out of respect for my dead friend and his surviving family, I will not divulge his name and only provide the facts of the case as was told to me.

I had not seen this friend in a long time, and we were able to reconnect some years back while preparing for my best friend's wedding. The night before the wedding, we had a dinner party at my best friend's house. As the evening wore down and people began to leave, the only ones left were my best friend, our now deceased friend, and myself. The friend in question had recently purchased a new firearm, a Desert Eagle, and was showing it to us. I complimented him about the piece, however I was wondering why he needed a gun. In retrospect perhaps I should have audibly posed that question and forced him to reason why he needed it.

After the wedding he went back to his state, and I did not hear from him again. Little did I know at that time I would never see him again.

Over the next three years or so, I would receive reports from my best friend on how our mutual friend was getting himself in trouble with the gun. I began to understand the psychological difference in the behavior of our friend and how the transformation was very similar to the depiction of power in an old hip hop song. In the song "I Gave You Power," written by Nas, it talks in detail about how having a gun for a young black man with low self-esteem gives him a sense of unmitigated power. However because of this sense of power the main character in the song makes some poor decisions and ultimately meets a tragic end. The fiction in the art is not very dissimilar from the reality of my mutual friend.

In December 2007, my best friend called me and informed me that our buddy was dead from a self-inflicted gunshot wound to his head. The details are sketchy, but as far as I know our mutual friend got into a very heated argument with his then pregnant girlfriend. From what we understand, these fights occurred often, and he had a history of pulling his gun on her in the past. According to the police, they had an ongoing record of domestic disputes between they couple. This final episode proved to be fatal for them both because during the argument, my mutual friend apparently pulled out his gun and killed his girlfriend in the heat of the moment. After a few moments, the reality of what he had done sank in as he looked at the lifeless corpse of his pregnant girlfriend. He had a series of choices to make and concluded he did not want to go to prison for the rest of his life. He called his sister and, speaking very rapidly and vaguely, told her he loved her and wanted to be cremated. He then turned the gun on himself and ended his own life.

I was in the process of writing this book when this tragedy transpired, I immediately related his ill-fated conclusion to issues with self-esteem and succumbing to negative emotions. With all due respect, my friend as a black man did not have the tools needed to elevate his self-esteem; he was probably suffering from some form of depression. The depression combined with the hard reality of trying to generate a decent living triggered the unstable emotions he experienced. He was of West Indian descent, which involved socialization to a certain cultural value system that may not necessarily adequately address improving the self-esteem from the individual standpoint of being a human being first. Finally, having a false sense of power from having that gun placed him in a mental and emotional state of warped confidence with which he was unwilling to part.

Please understand my perspective. I am very saddened by the loss of my friend. Despite the circumstances of his death, he was a great individual who valued hard work and friendship. However, it was a needless act that left three people dead. It could have been avoided by not having the gun in the first place, or confiding in his friends and perhaps turning to professional help when his life became too stressful.

I am not advocating for the process of deprogramming yourself to the levels of not feeling any emotion at all. Emotions do serve a purpose and remind us that we are human. Nonetheless, I am advocating for a controlled expression of our emotions that can be exercised under appropriate circumstances, followed by rational and logical decision making.

There are times in life when anger is an appropriate response to the situation. Sometimes we are faced with conditions that are beyond our control, and it provokes anger as a response. Feeling powerless as a black man in America can certainly emit feelings of anger; even Malcolm X talked about how he enjoyed his label as a demagogue and being the angriest black man in America. Nonetheless, I assert that anger should be used judiciously, and the response should meet the conditions of the circumstances. Most situations in life can be handled without anger or the need to intimidate or threaten someone else's well-being. As illustrated in the case of my friend and countless other tragedies of black men, anger can lead to clouded judgment, poor decision making, and tragic results.

What I want to convey is that negative emotional pain is a Western socialized behavior. From birth we are inculcated with emotional psychological triggers, which are activated by certain stimuli from the outside milieu. This is symptomatic of a Western culture that instills the responses of guilt, in the form of Sigmund Freud's super ego. Nonetheless, just as we are socialized by it, we can un-socialize ourselves from this influence.

For the most part we learn negative emotional reactions from our parents and other influential adults. In addition, when we enter the community and witness a dispute, as young ones we are influenced by how the other members in our community settle their conflicts; oftentimes for blacks it is through violence. Naturally we grow up thinking this is the appropriate way to respond and handle conflict. Not until years later, when we are told we could just ignore it and walk away, do we realize we have a choice. In some cases it is too late. The point is that our emotional response to any given situation is a choice, and we are obligated to have the right to take control of ourselves.

In the black community we have a warped concept of respect and what it means. Too many of us, it translates into what's known as street cred(ibility). Because of this dangerous value system, we place ourselves in compromising situations that can be extremely detrimental. We need to actively improve our self-esteem, independent of any contingency on negative values from the community to create better options for ourselves.

How We Use Our Past against Us

The topic of our own personal past and how we use it against ourselves is a very important subject for me, on several different levels. I must be responsible and honestly admit that throughout my life, I have allowed and used the negative memories of my life incorrectly, to the prolonged detriment of the development of my self-esteem.

Jerry Minchinton says,

> As human beings, we have the unique ability to consciously recall memories with great clarity. We replay some of them so vividly they almost seem to be happing again. We abuse this talent by bringing the past into the present more often than we should. The problem

then lies with us and how we use this remarkable ability to recall strong memorization. Moreover, the problem is we tend to focus our attention more on unpleasant recollections and in remembering them subjecting ourselves once again to their punishing emotional blows.

When we experience negative or unpleasant events especially really traumatic ones, we may find them hard to forget. Because we generate such intense feelings in response to them, our emotion-charged memories seem to take on a life of their own. With a morbid sort of fascination, we replay these painful recollections again and again in our minds. We remind ourselves of every detail, we feel the injury anew, and we re-experience the hurt and the emotional turmoil we felt, sometimes with even greater intensity than originally.

Although this kind of mental review may seem harmless, in fact, it is just the opposite. This is because distressing experiences like this have one thing in common: in all of them we cast ourselves in the role of the victim. When we react to an incident with intense negative energy, it is because we feel weak, helpless, and unable to defend or protect ourselves from someone or something we consider bigger and/or more powerful. The more we remind ourselves of painful circumstances like these, the less we respect ourselves. Without exception, they add to our feelings of inadequacy by emphasizing our lack of power and control.

It is not the experience itself that makes us feel awful; it is the way we perceive it and how we respond to it.

If particular situations from the past seem extremely disturbing, it is time to re-consider them, to try to see them differently than before. No matter what kind of experiences we may have had, or how distressing or awful they seemed when they happened, we are free to re-evaluate them whenever we choose and learn to see them in a less harmful way.

If I deliberately refuse to entertain painful memories and stop providing them with emotional fuel, they will lose their power to disturb me. In addition, my feelings about any part of my life depend on which memories I choose to emphasize, rather than the actual events that occurred then. I can change the quality of my life by choosing to stress pleasant memories.

I explained the lives of my parents and their socialized behavior, and in turn how it affected my brothers and me. I illustrated how I hated my mother growing up, and for the most part I can only recall negative memories about my experiences with my family. I say this because I am by no means a finished product; I still struggle with my self-esteem at times. However I know that it is an ongoing journey of mental and emotional self-improvement to reach and successfully maintain self-love despite what is going on in my life. Remember, true self-esteem is when you can still love and have confidence in yourself and your abilities during challenging times.

At times when I was younger, I enjoyed being the victim. In my undeveloped sense of self, I thought that people would have compassion for me, as expressed in the Western, romanticized fictitious way, and it would allow me not to be held to the same standards of personal responsibility and accountability. Later on in my life, as a teenager and a young adult, I willingly saw myself a victim whenever I felt betrayed by friends and lovers, when things in my life did not pan out as I wanted. Even as recent as my late thirties, I very often used the negative past to generate arguments with my mother during our phone calls. Nonetheless, the events were in the past, and therefore she could do nothing to effectively atone for them. But I used the past as a form of retaliation, to purposely hurt her the same way I felt she hurt me growing up. I am embarrassed to admit that this emotionally charged tennis match went on for more than a decade in my adulthood. However with each mental recollection of a negative experience with my mother, I actually weakened my own self-esteem.

As I began to study the empowering concepts of self-esteem improvement, I adopted the tools needed to gradually move away from viewing myself as a victim and began practicing more self-empowering techniques for my life.

Minchinton concludes,

> If the past events still influence me, it is not because they must but because I choose to let them. Except for what we can learn from it, the past is unimportant because it no longer exists. The only period of time with any value, and the only time for which we are truly responsible, is *right now*, this present moment. To the degree we direct our attention to the past, we make it unavoidable for use in the here and now. Only by opening ourselves fully to the present can we effectively deal with it. And only by deliberately turning away from the past can we

avoid being in a position where, instead of savoring the present moment to the fullest, we are still nibbling on the undigested memories of the past.

What can I learn from my past? It's simple: what not to do in the future. Every mistake I have made in my life, I make the utmost attempt to learn from it in order to not repeat it and to improve. I have plenty of experience to work from: from not performing well academically in my first years of college, to not doing well in my first jobs as a professional in the workforce, to being a bad boyfriend on many occasions, I have made marginal to terrible mistakes in my life. However, eventually I did improve to become an outstanding student, I significantly augmented my job performance, and I placed a high value on being a good husband. Subsequently, I consciously work every day to fulfill my role with dignity and integrity at being the best husband I am capable of being.

With respect to my parents' past mistakes and how it affected me. truthfully it was very traumatic growing up the way I did. However with a broader understanding of their lives and the impact of American history against them. I can understand why they made the decisions they made. I do not agree because I honestly believe if I were in that circumstance, I would have made different decisions. But that is speculation at best. and I know this. You never really know what you would do if you were in a certain circumstance; you can only hope that you would make the best decisions.

Nonetheless, it does not make me a better person if I continue to hold onto the negativity of my childhood experiences. I have since learned to turn that energy onto motivation to achieve goals that even I did not believe I was capable of achieving. More important, my past experiences have no realistic impact on who I am today; I do not allow it to affect my self-esteem. I am not my past, and the only value it can have is the value I permit it.

In the case of evaluating America and her historical crimes and active racism against African Americans, I certainly would not advocate forgetting that. I urge you to not let the pain of the past or current racism stop you on your path to success. That past is real, it hurts, and based on the way a large percentage of us live our lives, it still affects us. The objective should be to use that unique history as motivation to not only to be the best we can be individually, but also to add significant contributions to our already rich history.

We can derive some strong lessons from the Jewish community on how they prepared themselves for success. They never forget their past as victims of a criminal act. The ethnoreligious consciousness has helped them not only achieve success but sustain it for generations. As a community we can enjoy the same amount of stability and success. We can overcome our personal dislike and hatred for being black, transforming that into self-pride and personal responsibility to improve our lives.

Understand that we do not have to think alike or be dogmatic to the same vision of every black person. The black community is not a monolith, and no one has the same ideas about a particular issue. However I do see the big picture and believe that when one of us makes it, we all can achieve the same level of success. It really does not matter what particular political party you belong to, what religion you subscribe to, or what social economic background you come from. When we at least acknowledge that we are black and successful, there is inspiration for the rest of us. We have a great future ahead. In order to reach it with both hands, we must let go of the past and grasp the opportunities of the future that our self-esteem creates for us.

Why Am I Here, and What Does My Life Mean?

I just finished watching the conclusion of *Roots: The Next Generations,* and the ending struck me like a bolt of lightning, leaving me emotional and in tears. In the story of the original *Roots,* author Alex Haley successfully traces back his own family history all the way back to Africa. He begins with the first captured African, Kunta Kinte, and his voyage across the Atlantic Ocean. Kinte was sold as a slave, and thus began the long line of Africans born in America as slaves, up until the Emancipation Proclamation.

Roots: The Next Generations starts with Kunta Kinte's great great grandson, Tom Harvey, during the segregated time of Jim Crow, and it ends with Haley going back to Africa and finding his ancestral lineage with the Mandingo Mandika tribe. He was in a village where he met an old African griot, who dictated the history of the Mandika from the beginning of the Mali civilization during the sixteenth century. During the presentation of the griot, Haley interrupted him when he mentioned Kunta Kinte as the oldest son of his father who went out to find a log for a drum and was never seen again by family because he was captured by the slave catchers.

Haley excitedly jumped up and connected the dots: that was the same story he heard as a little boy growing up. He finally exclaims with happiness, "I found you, old African!" After that the griot formally welcomes him in the Mandika clan, and all of the villagers embrace him.

That that was the most beautiful thing I ever saw, and I began to cry out of joy and sorrow. The joy was for the success of Alex Haley having come from such a strong and proud family history that neither slavery nor Jim Crow could take away. He also spoke about times earlier in his life when he struggled to find his way because he was looking for meaning and a purpose. He was able to find it in writing and ultimately discovered that one of his purposes was to connect the family full circle from Africa to slavery to Jim Crow to civil rights, and then back to Africa.

However I was sad for myself because in all frankness, I did not come from such a proud family heritage. I can only go as far back as my grandmother, and at present she suffers from Alzheimer's. My mother never took us to family reunions, and I never really met any relatives from my father's side; I never met my paternal grandmother. In addition, the chaos that plagued my family since I was a kid was so embarrassing that a lot of times I wished I belonged to someone else's family.

In a lot of cases, white people can get along just fine without a strong knowledge of their history or personal heritage. However this assertion is radically different for African Americans. I assert that it is more imperative for us to have a real sense of our personal history, to help foster strong self-esteem and provide a compass for the direction of our lives.

My parents did not have attributes such as dignity or integrity. My father was a hustler and my mother was a welfare cheat, and there were never any heart-filled stories about the olden days and how our family struggled to persevere with integrity under the most difficult of circumstances. My mother believed in all the white man's inhuman imagery about the African race and was very willing to disconnect herself from the heritage and the ideological community. Although she was an unemployed hustler and a cheat herself, she never wanted to identify as someone of the black community.

All I know is that my mother is from Goldsboro, North Carolina, and my father is from Richmond, Virginia. By the way they both viewed and lived their lives, it is clear that any level of pride and family integrity or oral heritage was stripped away long before they were born by the intensity of the criminal white racist social structure of the time. By the time my brothers and I were born, neither of them had any concept of family, black pride, or responsibility.

As a result I never grew up with any family pride, and like Alex Haley, I was always searching for something to give my life purpose. I admired how my childhood friends were proud and close to their families, and I longed for that type of family connection. When I was old enough to travel by myself, about twelve, I always wanted to be with my friends more. As a kid I hated to be with my family.

When I went away to college, I read the autobiography of Malcolm X, and that led to other reading about my heritage and history. My education in the philosophy of Black Power gave me my pride, my identity, and a sense of purpose that my parents could not. Black Power became and still is a big part of my self-esteem; it gives me a sense of purpose by filling the holes in my family history to understand why my parents forgot or never knew who they are. Because of the civil rights movement, I had life-improving advantages that they did not. Because of that, it allowed me to pursue the intellectual understanding of my family history in a roundabout way.

The meaning of true self-esteem is to unconditionally value oneself regardless of one's socioeconomic background—or in my case, knowledge of personal family history. True self-esteem is to have internal confidence in who you are, not just in good times but during the bad times that everyone experiences. True self-esteem means when you unconditionally love yourself, you can love others; in my case, I found a way to forgive my parents.

I do know this much about family pride: It starts with me. It is my responsibility to pass it down to the next generation of the Smith family. As a married man, it is my responsibility to nurture the self-esteem of my children and teach them the proud heritage of the African American community as a component to their self-esteem.

The Election of Barack Obama and What It Means to Blacks and America in General

The election of America's first African American president, Barack Obama, is a significant and powerfully historical event. This is the culmination of the efforts of African

Americans' and mostly college-age liberal whites' ideas and endeavors to make the right decision to vote in the best candidate.

During the fist six months since the outcome of the November presidential election, it appeared as if the racism in America was on the decline. With some obvious exceptions, this assertion is true. When we analyze the demographics of the people who voted, it is clear that whites are significantly less racist than prior generations. For example, population wise, over 95 percent of African American voted for Obama, but we are only 14 percent of the country. White Americans comprise up to 70 percent of the country; therefore even though most African Americans voted for Obama, its population is still too small to significantly affect the overall electoral outcome. Over 43 percent of whites, mostly college aged, voted for Obama along with about half of the voting Latino population. This is what solidified his amazing victory over John McCain.

Over a year or so later, America has experienced a significant level of white backlash. White backlashes are not unusual during moments of apparent African American progress. After the 1865 Emancipation Proclamation that freed American Blacks from slavery, whites rose up in defiance of the liberating act. With a series of heated and sometimes violent confrontations, the initial white backlashes led to the assassination of Abraham Lincoln and eventually the start of Jim Crow segregation. After the success of the civil rights movement, led by Martin Luther King Jr., the white backlash led to the assassinations of President John F. Kennedy and Dr. King. Some fifteen years later, the backlash created the ultraconservative and perceived anti-black policies of the Reagan administration.

I assert that white backlash comes from the ever-growing reality of the declining significance of being white. I'll explain it this way: As mentioned earlier in the text, the very same institutions, philosophies, practices, and religions that socialized and inculcated a black inferiority complex helped to elevate the esteem and stature of being white along with all the social, economic, and political privileges that accompany it. There is a large percentage of poor whites that lives below the poverty line in America; it is safe to assert that they are struggling and are unhappy about their economic circumstances, as would anyone else in poverty. However, there is a bit of a different psychosis about the reality of their existence. The common statement for most poor whites is, "I may be poor, but I'm not black."

Anti-racist and political correspondent Tim Wise does a brilliant job of explaining the origins of white-skinned privilege and how it affected poor whites. Wise maintains that in earlier American colonial times, the white elites had similar disdain for the poor white labor class as they did for the first African slaves during that time; neither labor class had power. However, they were always viewed as a threat to rise up against the elites once they understood that their common plight and enemy. The elite class understood this potentially precarious situation and allowed the poor labor whites to have and maintain some privileges, such as small amounts of land and a certain level of social status. The elites allowed the poor white to exert social power and control over the African slave class. Finally, they understood that they could financially benefit by helping to keep the slaves in order. Over time this formulated the ideology of white-skinned privilege and the feeling of acceptance of being poor and powerless against the rich class but still being above the poor African slave class.

In fact the reason why poor whites historically left their home European countries to go to the Americas was to seek fortune, try to become a part of the elite, and enjoy a higher social status than that of the black slave class. It was common knowledge in those days that if you immigrated to the one of the colonies or metro poles of your mother country, as a white person you had a better chance of achieving economic success than the black slave population already present. It was the centuries old divide-and-conquer trick, and it worked beautifully. Later it would be just as effective when applied to light—and dark-skinned blacks and newly arrived labor groups such as the Italians, Jews, and Irish. These groups all had in common the social repression from the American elites, but because they were accepted as whites, they too took up the social position to become racist against the American black class regardless of their socioeconomic status. This ideology provided them with a basic level of self-esteem that African Americans did not have, and combined with no legal or social barriers to thwart their progress, eventually these group ascended to middle-class status. Nonetheless, understand that some of these groups did face intense prejudice and were on occasion the target of violent attacks in America. But that is significantly different than having actual laws and acts of violence aimed specifically at a single group for the purpose of disenfranchising them.

The election of Barack Obama does provide African American inspiration and perhaps a basic level of self-esteem, just as the elites did for the poor whites. And because of the "Obama effect," I hypothesize that over the next five to ten years, America will experience a surge in successful college—and professional-trained African Americans ready to competently enter the American workforce.

Remember, the heart of the American sociological problem, despite its racial history, is—and will always be—labor. When the country has a surplus of workers and not enough livable wage jobs to accommodate the workers, high levels of unemployment occur, which creates frustration and opens the door to the scapegoating of other ethnic and racial groups. No politicians or labor leaders actively attack the major corporations or the elites that helped to develop the conditions to begin with; instead they go after groups against which they feel they can win.

When poor whites feel that they have to compete with other groups for a scarcity of livable wage jobs, and the purest principle of the best person fit for the job is applied (and it's not based on skin color), without self-esteem and an adequate level of education in the history of American labor practices, poor whites will feel disenfranchised and create the backlash.

Even some white Latinos that enjoy white-skinned privilege are perturbed at the new level of societal openness for opportunities. They feel that their social status of being white is somehow less prestigious. It was rumored that after Obama had won the election, someone called in on one of the popular Latino talk radio shows and commented, "Now blacks will think they are hot shit."

White backlash dies hard, because without a genuine sense of self-esteem and love for who they are as a human beings, ethnocentrism and just being white are not enough armaments to give someone the confidence they need to successfully compete in a changing America.

Conclusion

I love my life, and I love my existence. I love the fact that I exist, and I accept the responsibility that the quality of my life depends on my ability to create the life I want. I accept the responsibility and consequence of every decision I make; this makes me very powerful because I can control my every action. You should understand and accept the reality and responsibility that the quality of your life is dependent on you.

I accept the fact that I have a magnificent brain, and my ability to think will dictate the level of my success. I accept the fact that no one is coming to save me and that my life is my responsibility in and of itself. As I stated before, this is a powerful reality, and I appreciate it because it makes clear that I must act and perform in a conscious manner for my life, not relying on anything outside of myself for salvation. No one is coming to save me. Your life is entirely your responsibility. Once you understand how profound this concept and feeling is, you are that much more liberated and can thus act accordingly.

I will protect and defend my life at all costs. I will secure my brain and my thoughts against any doctrine, political or economic system, law or code, or philosophy aimed at undermining my existence. If these doctrines do not celebrate me and my right to live, they are an unnecessary waste of time from which I cannot benefit. I am better apt to studying concepts that celebrate my life and teach an appreciation of humanity. As Malcolm X once stated, "Any philosophy that teaches you to not defend or protect your life is a criminal philosophy." Some of these philosophies and religions only preach about the death of life. Those doctrines are incongruent with our physical reality. We must learn to effectively develop coping mechanisms to help us deal with the reality of life.

I place the statements in clear terms such as these because I want everyone to understand the simple fact that your life belongs to you and no one else. Celebrate your life and use the philosophy of smart decision making to guide your direction. Do not accept anything less of yourself in any of your endeavors, and realize that your brain is a magnificent tool that, when used appropriately, can maximize your natural talents and in many cases surpass and surprise you on what you are capable of doing.